MW01257236

Bungalow Kid

Bungalow Kid

A Catskill Mountain Summer

Philip Ratzer

excelsior editions
State University of New York Press
Albany, New York

Published by State University of New York Press, Albany

© 2010 State University of New York

For information, contact State University of New York Press, Albany, NY
www.sunypress.edu

Excelsior Editions is an imprint of State University of New York Press

Production by Eileen Meehan
Marketing by Fran Keneston

Library of Congress Cataloging-in-Publication Data

Ratzer, Philip.
    Bungalow kid : a Catskill Mountain summer / Philip Ratzer.
        p. cm.
    ISBN 978-1-4384-3300-4 (pbk. : alk. paper)
    1. Ratzer, Philip—Childhood and youth.   2. Jewish children—New
York (State)—Catskill Mountains—Biography.   3. Jews—New York
(State)—Catskill Mountains—Biography.   4. Bungalows—New York
(State)—Catskill Mountains—History—20th century.   5. Summer
resorts—New York (State)—Catskill Mountains—History—20th century.
6. Catskill Mountains (N.Y.)—Social life and customs—20th century.
7. Catskill Mountains (N.Y.)—Biography   8. Jews—New York (State)—
New York—Biography.   I. Title.

F127.C3R35 2010
974.7'35043092—dc22
[B]   2009051683

10 9 8 7 6 5 4 3 2 1

To my parents, Bernie and Millie Ratzer,
who made all these memories possible

To my wife, Mary, whose encouragement, support,
and love made this book a reality

Contents

1

Worlds Apart

Not too long ago, it was 1958, not the year it is now. In my neighborhood in the Bronx, as the days lengthened and the weather became warmer, my friends and I had begun to play stickball, punchball, and even baseball again, even though both the Giants and the Dodgers had abandoned New York for California, which we were still pretty miffed about. The girls, meanwhile, were all twirling their hula hoops, sometimes several at a time, which was very impressive, though from our point of view, pretty dumb, and we told them so. We were all anxious about Elvis going in the Army, though we continued to listen to his songs on the radio, along with the Everly Brothers, Ricky Nelson, and Jerry Lee Lewis. Just about everyone I knew saw *The Blob* in the movies, and we loved watching *American Bandstand* on TV. And despite the awful headlines in the newspaper practically every day, there was no doubt that spring was slowly turning into summer, and from my particular vantage point, life was good.

I was putting the finishing touches on my elementary school education, completing sixth grade with a few hundred of

1

my learned colleagues. We had recently received our treasured autograph books, mementos of six years of academic achievement, and would pass them around the room to garner as many autographs and words of wisdom as possible before class actually began. This continued in the cafeteria as well, sometimes at a fevered pitch, the autograph books getting far more attention than the food du jour.

When I came across my autograph book recently, it had not seen the light of day for more years than I care to remember, but I accidentally rediscovered it during a search for a totally unrelated item in a dark, spider-webbed corner of the garage. But there it was, staring up at my unbelieving eyes out of the gloom—a little book with multicolored pages bound in a red, white, and blue leatherette cover, marked, in what used to be bright gold, *Public School 90*.

For a moment, I knew what archaeologists experience uncovering a find from another time. I blew off the dust, wiped it clean of years of disuse, and opened the book to my world of fifty years before. There was my school, three stories of brick and glass, in a photo probably taken when it was built in 1920 something. My principal, Peter J. DiNapoli was next, a man I had never actually seen in real life. I flipped several pages ahead. Names and faces long forgotten came suddenly to life, as did the personalities, often reflected in the classic witticisms expressed on the various pages by my sixth-grade cohorts—

> If you get married and have a divorce,
> Come to my stable and marry my horse.
> —Bobby Becker

Some pages were dated "till meatballs bounce," or "till Niagara Falls." One page, back at the beginning, was entitled "My Favorites," designed to provide an encapsulated profile of the book's owner: TV Show: *Ramar of the Jungle* . . . Song: "Little Darling" . . . Movie: *Apemen from Space* . . . Sport: Stickball. I was obviously an urban sophisticate, even way back then.

My official photo showed a confident, smiling, skinny kid with curly dark hair, a reasonably pleasant face, trim white shirt, and his father's tie. What the photo didn't reveal was that I was always the tallest kid in the class, something that junior high school kids would soon teach me to be ashamed of. I continued to thumb through the autograph book, each page a different color, and holding a different endearment, like

> Don't worry if your job is small and your rewards
>   are few,
> Remember that the mighty oak was once a nut like
>   you.
>
> —Sandy Klein

All the pages that carried actual dates showed early June, 1958. Then there were several blank pages, and a continuation about a month or more later. At first this confused me, but looking at the various signatures revealed the explanation for the time gap—the pages were inscribed and signed by my summertime friends, with whom I would reacquaint myself each summer. My parents had been renting a bungalow in upstate New York ever since I was an infant, and each year, for part of June, all of July and August, and even a bit of September, I resided in a world as far removed from the asphalt and concrete of the Bronx as a kid could imagine.

And there before me were the utterances of my friends from Pesekow's Bungalow Colony, being read for the first time in half a century. It was absolutely fascinating, and it took me back through the years. Most of the pages contained similarly silly couplets in faded ink or pencil, and the names, Melanie Pesekow, Ray Gottlieb, Marty Rosenfeld, and Sarah Steinway were immediately recognizable, even though we saw each other for only three months a year. Marty's inscription,

> When you get married and think you're sweet,
> Take off your shoes and smell your feet

was exceptionally inspirational, matching his personality perfectly. The last page was Sarah's, and her message, in pencil, took on a somewhat different tone—

Remember Grant, remember Lee,
But most of all, remember me.

Just beneath her name, she'd added a very unusual suggestion: *Read "Isle of View."* Though I read a lot, I had never heard of that particular book, but I recall promising myself to check the local library when I got back to the Bronx. I recall as well that it took me quite a while to fully understand what Sarah was actually saying to me in her coded message. Holding her page open before me, I did indeed remember her, and so much more. I find it interesting that my recollections of the winters, the school years, are essentially vague and inconsistent. But those of the summers in The Country are as vivid as yesterday, and that particular summer of 1958 would be especially meaningful in a way I couldn't even begin to imagine as I entered my classroom on a balmy morning in early June. As for now, I found it incredibly easy to bring it all back, to return to The Country, to, as Sarah suggested, *"remember."*

What we called The Country back then was a faraway place, so far from the steamy streets of the Bronx that it seemed like we were indeed traveling to another world entirely. In it were towns and villages that to me had magical names; they were places that even today still suggest a certain fairytale quality when I see or hear their names: Monticello, Woodridge, Mountain Dale, Fallsburg, Liberty, Loch Sheldrake: it was the realm of Sullivan County, New York. In it were sun-filled green meadows and dark, mysterious woods; wonderful lakes and streams for endless summer fun; enough frogs, fish, snakes, salamanders, and turtles to keep any kid deliriously happy; there were cool, starry nights and dewy mornings; and there was the special charm of a childhood summer romance. It was The Country.

Or, as some would have it, The Mountains. No matter. What mattered was that it existed somewhere out there beyond the George Washington Bridge. I was thinking about The Country that morning in June of 1958, as I sat in my classroom seat waiting for the right moment to give Mrs. Grable the paper I was clutching in my hand, occasionally being distracted by the need to sign someone's autograph book. I shoved my own inside my desk when I saw Mrs. Grable enter the room. How well I remember being a kid of distinction in my Bronx school, looked upon with unconcealed envy when I brought that important document, the note from my mother, to class, requesting that I be allowed to leave school weeks before the school year actually ended so that I might travel upstate with my family to spend the summer in The Country. I proudly (and somewhat conceitedly) got up from my seat in the back of the room as soon as Mrs. Grable sat down at her desk. I walked up to the front of the room and handed her the sacred note. There was a brief whiff of her perfume, which somehow reminded me of my Aunt Molly's bathroom; I then returned to my seat, foolishly thinking that the deed was done. My ticket out was about to be validated. But looking up from my mother's note, Mrs. Grable, her eyes bright with the anticipation of an impromptu learning experience, said "Boys and girls, Philip will be leaving our class soon to travel upstate with his family for the summer." Then, turning directly to me, "Philip, why don't you tell the class all about Lake Sheldon."

All of a sudden, the pride and conceit were gone, replaced by the nervousness of having to stand next to my seat to address the class. Being as tall as I was, the movement always made me feel like a giraffe getting back up after a drink in some African pond. Every kid in the room turned around and stared at me, eagerly awaiting my stirring oration.

"Um, uh, well, it's really called Loch Sheldrake, and it's in the country. We have this bungalow, and we go up there every summer." I started to sit back down, hoping that my eloquence overwhelmed Mrs. Grable, and would suffice. But she wanted more, asking "What do you do there?"

Standing next to my seat again, I said, "Well, lots of stuff. We go swimming in the lake a lot, we go fishing, exploring.

Lots of stuff." I quickly sat back down, hoping that would end the proceedings, which it indeed did, as Mrs. Grable, frustrated in her efforts to turn my request for early dismissal into something greater, let the opportunity pass. Relieved to be seated once again, I saw that Neil, immediately to my left, was glaring at me, muttering just barely audibly, "Lucky stiff." No argument there. I briefly turned my attention to the front of the room, but I knew that the door to summer vacation had already partially opened. My thoughts were not on Mrs. Grable's lesson, but on returning to The Country. A furtive glance out the open window and into the warm June morning called to my inner self. In a quick succession of mental images, I thought of my new PF Flyer sneakers, my fishing rod, the lake, the woods, and my summertime friends. Nothing within the confines of P.S. 90 could compete with that. Just send my report card to Pesekow's Bungalow Colony, Loch Sheldrake, New York. The first step had been taken. The journey was almost underway.

That Friday's walk home down the McClellan Street hill was filled with the realization that I wouldn't be taking this particular walk ever again. Sixth grade, in fact all elementary school, with its finger paints, white paste, bathroom "accidents," and nurturing teachers, was now behind me. I had cleaned out my desk, and Mrs. Grable promised to mail my report card and my research paper on Peru to Loch Sheldrake by the end of the month. Next fall, I'd be taking an entirely different walk, actually much shorter, to J.H.S. 22, just down the street from our apartment. But that was eons away, and not a real subject for concern. Yet.

Entering our first-floor apartment on College Avenue that day was like entering Allied Headquarters just before D-Day. My mother was General Eisenhower, the military uniform replaced by her floral print apron covering a house dress. There were cartons everywhere, clothing hanging in doorways, open suitcases on the beds, and pots and pans on the kitchen table. My mother, though she was in no mood for small talk, and deep into the tension and fatigue of the day before departure, was well aware that I had crossed a major bridge that day, and despite the chaos of packing, smiled as I came in the door and asked, "So? How was?"

"Pretty good," I responded, "I'm all set."

"Did you clean out your desk?"

"Yeah. This is everything I had."

"What about the address for Pesekow's? And my note? She has them, right?"

"Yeah, I gave that stuff to her on Tuesday."

"Okay. Why don't you take out whatever things you want to bring. I already packed your clothes."

For me, this meant the basic essentials for living in The Country: a select but small group of comic books, a rubber-banded stack of baseball cards, all my fishing gear, my basket-ball, my baseball glove, a Pensy Pinky for handball, and all the cash I could gather, which this year amounted to $4.33, mostly in coins, some of which I scooped out from under my bed.

Getting the car ready was something that occurred in the world of my father. At the time, I had no idea, but looking back on it, he must have had the car checked and rechecked from bumper to bumper. After all, we were talking about a trip of well over a hundred miles, and the car had to be ready to make this trip once a week for the next few months. But on the night before actually getting underway, the car was ready, gleaming and spotless as usual, inside and out. Packing the car was my mother's domain, and woe to anyone who got in her way. Think of it: the very survival of the family, far from the haunts of civi-lization, was her responsibility. She had to insure that we had everything we might need for the next two-and-a-half to three months—all the clothing, kitchen utensils, bedding, bathroom supplies, swimming paraphernalia, and food for when we got there, not to mention some food for the trip itself, for relying on road food, as far as she was concerned, was like playing with fire—far too dangerous to even contemplate. Somehow, amid all the excitement, yelling, arguing about what can and can't be brought along, my father convinced that it won't all fit in the trunk and the back seat around me and my sister, futilely repeating that anything forgotten will just have to wait until the following week, somehow, the job is completed and we're ready to go, with stern warnings that it will be an early departure in the morning.

Which it absolutely would be. After a quick breakfast in the kitchen, we started our morning ritual. With the sun low on the horizon, the street of apartment houses was in dark shadows. Since it was Saturday, we were the only sign of life on the entire block. A row of parked cars stretched along both sides of the street; only ours had all the doors and the trunk opened, the four of us rapidly carrying out last-minute items to be somehow stuffed into the few remaining air pockets left inside. In a little while, the door to the apartment was locked, we all got into our assigned places in the car, and with my father's words, "Okay, we're on our way," we pulled away from the curb. Later, my friends would be congregating across the street in the playground to determine the course of action for the day—movies, basketball, stick ball, punch ball, or just hanging out. Except that today would be different. It would all happen without me. I was on my way to nirvana. I would keep in touch with them by way of occasional letters and postcards, but as I looked out the back window of the car at the rapidly receding street, I knew that we would be worlds apart.

For me, this first leg of the trip was generally characterized by a suggested return to slumber, not easy when a third of the back seat, that area between me and my sister Sheila, was occupied by a short stack of cartons topped by a noisy birdcage containing our green and yellow parakeet, Peppy. If I did nod off, having slept a total of about twenty minutes the night before, I would usually awaken to the sound of the car crossing the George Washington Bridge. There was a different sound to the pavement, or maybe it was the height of the bridge above the Hudson River, or the way sound played through the suspension cables. Somehow, it was different. Maybe it was the difference of New Jersey. As we'd pass through the toll booths and pay the twenty-five-cent toll, we knew we were in a foreign land. The signs were different. The roadsides were different. Crowded apartment buildings quickly gave way to a varied assortment of gas stations, diners, tourist cabins, motels, and drive-up stores of every description. Some that defied description. Even the road itself had a different look. It was Route 17, one concrete lane in each direction that we would follow for the next few hours, all the way to the Promised Land.

I remember that around this point in the trip, it used to be time for our first on-the-road meal. That was a few years ago when I was just a little kid, and I would announce that I was hungry. My mother would break out the fresh rye bread, and make sandwiches for everyone. At that time in my life, my diet consisted entirely of rye bread and grape jelly. It took just a moment for the sandwich to be handed over the seat back to my anxious hands. Drinks came from a large canister with a spigot at the bottom, and was usually a sweet red fruit punch. My mother had what amounted to a small kitchenette at her seat. I don't know how she managed it, but she did. It wouldn't take long for my next announcement to be made, which was that I had to go to the bathroom. My father's response would usually be, "Okay. We'll be at the Red Apple soon, so hold it in." I'd respond, "I'll try," which always carried the suggestion that I might make it, but then again, I might not. I always felt, and still do, that it didn't hurt to negotiate from a position of at least perceived power.

For miles along this section of Route 17, we were seeing huge billboards along the road proclaiming RED APPLE REST—25 MILES, followed shortly by RED APPLE REST—22 MILES, and so on. The Red Apple, in Southfields, New York, was known far and wide by all those heading to or from The Country as *the* place to stop, and probably the only place to stop, on the entire trip. We never ate there. In fact, just about the only thing we ever did there was go to the bathroom. Those who ran the place were well aware that that was the main attraction, painting a gigantic sign, in huge blue letters on a white background, REST ROOMS, with an equally huge arrow pointing directly to the way in. Even this early in the season, hundreds of people milled about the acres of parking lots, some anxiously following that huge arrow, others heading for the restaurant itself, which had both indoor seating and outdoor service windows for hungry travelers. Above all, a giant red rooftop apple gleamed in the midmorning sun. My father had pulled up to the gas pumps, and had asked for his usual "Two bucks worth of high test." Before long, relieved and refreshed, we were all back in the car, returning to Route 17, quickly approaching and just as quickly leaving such places as Harriman, Monroe, and Goshen.

Somewhere in the rural farm country beyond Middletown, Route 17 began a long, slow, steady climb up the Shawangunk Mountains, which separated the relatively mundane world of Orange County from the paradise found in neighboring Sullivan County. It was known as the Bloomingburg Hill. There was no way around it. A new road was being built nearby that would soon change all this, but for now, it had to be climbed. My father was currently driving a 1957 Mercury, painted two shades of pink; with its V-8 engine, the hill was a snap. But how well I recall driving up the same hill a few years before, in our 1950 Oldsmobile, which was already old when we bought it. We never knew for sure if the car would get to the top or not. My father would add to the drama by letting us know every few minutes that the temperature gauge needle was going up. Would the car make it without overheating? Tension built as the Oldsmobile struggled up the miles-long incline. My sister and I were absolutely silent, knowing that this was not a time to ask questions, complain, or make comments of any kind. Sheila was two years older than me, but not a bit more brave. Or foolish. As we ultimately approached the hamlet of Bloomingburg, we knew we were just about at the summit, and as far as the car was concerned, we were apparently okay. But the worst was yet to come. At the very top of the hill, the road went through a little underpass and seemed to lead directly over a cliff and out into the admittedly rarified air of Sullivan County. But what good would it be if we didn't survive to enjoy it? Our very lives were in the hands of my father, holding the steering wheel in a death grip, making sure to take the sharp right turn just before the precipice at a slow enough speed, so that nothing unexpected would take place. My sister and I were so scared here that since simply closing our eyes wasn't sufficient enough to shield us from potential disaster, we'd actually scrunch down onto the floor for extra protection. Finally, after an eternity of terror on the floor of the car, my father would sound the "all clear." Another trip over that mountain had successfully been accomplished. My father hadn't driven the Olds over the cliff after all. We would then be able to get up off the floor and open our eyes. We were in Sullivan County at last, and we would live to tell about it.

I smiled at the recollection, feeling quite self-satisfied that, this year, I wasn't afraid of the Bloomingburg Hill at all. As we slowly drove down the other side of the mountain, I looked out into the valley below to see the village of Wurtsboro shimmering in the early June sunshine. This was one of the first actual crossroads we'd pass through. Here, some travelers would turn off onto Route 209 and drive toward Ellenville, in nearby Ulster County, to seek their particular haven. But not us. With Wurtsboro and the mountain behind us, we continued on Route 17 to Monticello, the nexus of the county, and its largest city. Even though the actual summer season was still a few weeks away, the city was bustling with activity. The sidewalks were crowded with people, the streets filled with drivers looking for parking spaces; here was every kind of store and service imaginable. The marquee of the Rialto theatre proudly proclaimed to passersby that *Gigi* was now playing; beneath the marquee dangled a blue banner announcing the presence of air conditioning inside. At the Short Line bus depot nearby, crowds of people, most toting luggage, waited for the next bus to their destination. Not everyone had the luxury of traveling in their own car. At this time, we were searching the streets for a sign pointing the way to Route 42, for at Monticello we left Route 17, which continued on to Liberty, location of the fabled Grossinger's Resort. Monticello, of course, was the home of the nearby Concord Hotel, beloved by millions over the years, but not our style. Having found Route 42, we turned away from the crowds, and continued on our way.

Route 42 meandered over the countryside and found its way to South Fallsburg, not nearly as large as Monticello, but busy with people nevertheless. Stores and restaurants lined both sides of the street. My father pointed out Frank and Bob's, his favorite area restaurant, where he'd like to "grab a meal" sometime soon, maybe even tonight. Passing over the railroad tracks and the nearby train station, we soon left South Fallsburg behind us. It didn't take long for my mother to point out a sign by the right side of the road that said, simply, GREEN'S COTTAGES. This was a small bungalow colony where we used to stay, and where I spent the first summers of my life. I happened to be deep into thumb-sucking as a baby and toddler, which was a delightful, absorbing activity that for me actually involved both thumbs—one, of course, was planted firmly in my mouth; the other, however, was carefully stroking a soft, smooth, special piece of fabric that might have been part of a shirt, or a pair of pants. Now it just so happened that Mr. Green himself owned and wore a pair of khaki trousers that suited my needs perfectly, and as my mother told the story, I was attached to Mr. Green's pants wherever he went.

In a little while, we passed the Flagler Hotel, at the time ranked quite high in the world of luxury Catskill resorts. This meant we were approaching Fallsburg, just a little crossroads town named after the spectacular bouldered falls of the Neversink River. Oretsky's Garage was on the right, and my father never failed to look to see if he could spot his old buddy Moe Oretsky, the owner, and honk as he passed. But not this time. Crossing the intersection, we could see the Crossroads Restaurant, perched right above the falls so that its patrons could enjoy the view. Just down the side road near the old stone bridge over the Neversink was one of the more infamous local night spots, The Wonder Bar, known throughout the area for its incredibly wicked reputation and goings-on. However, of more interest to me was a dirt road just past the Wonder Bar and a sign indicating SCHIEKOWITZ'S BUNGALOW COLONY, with a red arrow pointing the way.

Schiekowitz's was where we stayed for a few summers after we outgrew Green's. The dirt road led off the highway through corn fields and then crossed a small brook with a wooden, white-washed bridge. If we kids were on the bridge when a car or, better, a truck was coming from, or going to the colony, we would hold on to the railing and "go for a ride," for the bridge trembled and shook under the weight of various vehicles. For a five- or six-year-old, it was a lot of fun. That dirt road then went up a small hill into the colony itself. We started out at Schiekowitz's in a single, crowded room in a large rooming house with a deep wrap-around porch. There was a shared bathroom down the hall, and a common kitchen in an adjacent building. Eventually, we moved up to a modest bungalow.

What I remember best about Schiekowitz's was the forest and the river. What was remarkable about the forest, other than its incredible depth, was the number of gigantic, glacial boulders found within its confines. They were famous among the kids: Mother Rock (pretty big), Father Rock (even bigger), and Whale Rock (biggest of all, and a real challenge to climb). The woods were great; always dark, kind of spooky, full of adventure. A well-worn path led from the colony down to the Neversink River, where we'd swim and fish for sunnies and perch from the large, flat boulders that lined the riverbank. As time progressed into the modern world of the 1950s, however, river swimming became passé; consequently, the Schiekowitzes added the wonder of an in-ground swimming pool. But with the pool came a long list of rules and regulations for use that caused considerable friction between the residents, my mother included, and Mrs. Schiekowitz, the chief rule enforcer. As a result, their first summer with a pool was our last summer as residents. We moved on.

As we did this morning, leaving Fallsburg and its memories in our wake. It was now just a few miles to Woodbourne, where we'd turn off 42 and onto Route 52, going up the hill toward Loch Sheldrake. Woodbourne was a nice little town settled along both sides of the same Neversink River. It was, however, dominated by the overbearing presence of the Sullivan County Correctional Facility, a somber regional prison whose presence on the hillside could not be ignored. Prisoners were often seen out in the fields around the prison tending various crops in the hot summer sun. It was always astonishing to see them out there, always hard at work, always watched over by mounted police with rifles across their saddles. One time, when we were driving by, I saw a group of prisoners standing by a barn near the road with their hands raised high in the air, and several mounted officers pointing their rifles directly at them. I didn't know what was going on, but I never forgot the sight.

The turn onto Route 52 was actually just before the village proper. The landmark was a Shell station right at the intersection at the bottom of the hill. We made the sharp left and drove away from Woodbourne and its prison. Persistent loud static on the radio that prevented us from listening to William B. Williams on WNEW told us that we were both very far from home, and very close to our destination. Soon we'd be passing the New Roxy Hotel on the right and, on the left, a glimpse of Lake Evans and the sprawling Evans Hotel beyond the lake in the distance. A black-and-white state highway marker read, in bold print, LOCH SHELDRAKE and, in smaller print underneath, LIBERTY, 5. We had arrived.

2

The Promised Land

The village of Loch Sheldrake was essentially a small collection of stores and restaurants hugging the shore of the beautiful lake that gave the place its name. We slowly drove through town, each of us anxiously looking around to see if anything had changed since last year. We saw that Herbie's Restaurant, Joe's Deli, Sekofsky's Department Store, and the Strand theatre (now playing: "Tammy and the Bachelor"; coming soon: "Gigi") were right where we left them. Across the street, Pesekow's Barber Shop and Beauty Parlor, its bricks painted a light blue that tourists couldn't miss, still occupied the busy corner where the other road came in from nearby Hurleyville. And just up from that corner we could see that Kove's General Store was still there and open for business, the sidewalk out front crowded with produce from local farms. Continuing along Route 52, I spotted Fried's Drug Store—important to me, for it was the best source of comic books, especially *Classics Illustrated*, in the area. Nearby was the town's synagogue, then Town and Country Fashions, the path to Max's boathouse, and Rosenblatt's Car Service and Esso station, sporting its jaunty HAPPY MOTORING! sign. All that was left was to drive the short distance to the bungalow colony.

Pesekow's had two driveways, and our bungalow was up by the road, right next to the first driveway and the sign, L. PESEKOW'S BUNGALOW COLONY. My father turned in, and parked the car half on the grass, facing down hill, right next to the bungalow. We hadn't been out of the car since the Red Apple, so we were all anxious to get out and stretch our legs. For me, opening the car door and stepping outside was a lot like Dorothy stepping out of the farm house and into Oz. I wasn't in the Bronx anymore. There was grass under my feet and trees everywhere. The air was scented by fresh-cut lawns, pine trees, and fields of wildflowers. I could see the lake, just visible between the bungalows further down the hill. Crows were calling from nearby treetops, and the sky was a shade of blue rarely seen above apartment house roofs. In these surroundings, our humble two room bungalow would become a castle of limitless luxury.

My father found the door unlocked, and we all went inside, eager to look around. Freshly painted and spotlessly clean, all was in place. Bungalow 19 was roughly L-shaped, part of it being the kitchen and my sister's sleeping area, the other part being the bedroom, with one double and one single bed, two dressers, a closet, and a small bathroom. We propped the screen door open and began unloading the car. My mother was anxious to air the place out, so we opened all the windows as well. To her delight, she noticed that the bungalow now had a new refrigerator, even larger than the one we had back home. The rest of the place was essentially the same, the kitchen painted a soft yellow, the bedroom pink, a very popular color at the time. After a dozen or so trips to the car, all was unloaded with the unpacking process well underway. It didn't take long for the bare mattresses to be covered with our own sheets and blankets, our towels set out in the bathroom, and Peppy's cage hung from its hook in the kitchen. The dresser drawers and bedroom closet were filled with clothing, and our home away from home was ready for the summer ahead.

After a quick lunch, I was allowed to take off and do whatever I wanted. I grabbed my basketball and headed downhill through the colony. Our bungalow was one of three on what was called "the hill." Just below were the remaining dozen or so bungalows, sheltered under a grove of massive pine trees. Some of the bungalows housed two families; others, like ours, one. All were faced with a tan and black faux-brick siding which suggested more solidity than probably existed. Still further down the hill toward the lake was the casino, the social center of the colony. It had a deck that wrapped completely around the lake side of the building, and inside was a large room with some booths, a small store, pinball machines, and a Wurlitzer Rock-Ola jukebox. An attached room was reserved for card playing and occasional bingo.

There was a pier extending into the lake next to the casino, and I walked onto its wooden planks to have a close look at the water. A school of minnows was darting this way and that in the shallows, their silver sides glinting in the sun. When I reached down into the cool water, they scrambled in all directions, to regroup a short distance away. Everything around me looked a lot like I remembered it from last time. It felt so good to be back.

Not many people were around, which I was more or less glad about. It was always a bit uncomfortable and unsettling the first few days back, not knowing who you'd see, what they'd look like, if they'd remember you. I headed over to the handball court and its adjacent basketball hoop. Next to it was a children's playground. As I looked around, I noticed some new additions I didn't quite like. One was a four-foot chain-link fence that ran all along the lakefront to the edge of the property. I thought it ugly, but concluded that it was probably installed for safety reasons, and necessary to keep little kids away from the lake. Then there was this tall steel pole set into the ground in concrete, with a yellow soccer style ball suspended from the top by a rope reaching about half way to the ground. I had no idea what it was or how it was played, but I would soon find out.

Shortly, a kid came down the hill from the bungalows to join me. He was wearing the first pair of shorts I had seen that year, his dirt-covered knees revealing that he had probably been creeping around under a bungalow or two. Since he was a few years younger, naturally I didn't acknowledge his existence, but continued to shoot baskets just as if he wasn't there. Undeterred, he suddenly shouted, "Remember last year?"

Not to encourage him too much, I just said, "Yeah."

"It was great, wasn't it?"

"Yeah."

"I'm Mark. Remember me?"

Okay, I decided to give the kid a break. "Sure," I said. "I'm Philip."

"I know. I remember you, too."

"Want to shoot a few?"

"Yeah!"

So we both shot a few baskets, during which time Mark gave a running account of all the high points and low points of the past year that he felt I should know about, including his run-in with the measles, his third-grade teacher, and his parents' divorce, which resulted in him having a new last name. I guess my level of interest wasn't quite what he expected, so after a while he decided that he'd better head back home; off he went, saying "See ya" as he trotted away.

I continued shooting on my own, and had become quite absorbed in an imaginary championship game when I heard someone approaching from behind. I turned and saw that it was my friend and sometime girlfriend, Melanie. She was the Pesekow's daughter, and lived in Florida in the off-season. As a result, she was deeply tanned, and smiled broadly as she approached.

"Hi, Philip! How are you?"

"Hi, Mel. I'm good. How are you?"

"Great. My mother told me you were coming today. When'd you get here?"

"A couple of hours ago. How about you? How long have you been here?"

"About two weeks."

"Two weeks! How come?"

"In Florida, school ends before Memorial Day, and besides, I get permission to leave early."

"Yeah, me too."

"Did you have a good winter?"

"Oh, you know. The usual, I guess. What about you?"

"It was okay."

"Is anyone else here?"

"I don't think so. A lot of people are coming up next weekend. I'm pretty sure Marty and Ray. Also Sarah. You remember Sarah, don't you?"

"Sure I do. Why wouldn't I?"

"Oh, nothing," she said, kind of smiling. "Just asking. By the way—did you see the tetherball?"

"The what?"

"Tetherball. Over there. Everybody's playing it in Florida. We even play it in gym."

So that's what it was. Melanie went on to explain how to play tetherball, which involved two people hitting the ball in opposite directions. She thought it was a wonderful game. I thought it was a game for morons, but I didn't let on. Girls like Melanie had come to play an increasingly important role in my life lately, and I didn't want to say anything that had even the slightest chance of hurting her feelings. So I kept my thoughts about tetherball a secret, at least for now. Just then, the colony's P.A. system came on, with an announcement we would hear at least fifty times over the course of the summer. The Pesekows had a microphone in their little casino store, and usually employed it either to call someone down to the colony's only phone booth to take a call, or to call Melanie:

"Melanie! Melanie come down to the casino. Melanie come down."

So Melanie said she had to go, and we both said that we'd see each other later. It was wonderful seeing her again. Things were already beginning to pick up right where they left off the year before. As I watched her run back to the casino, I thought about how much taller she was than last year, and definitely prettier. Her eyes were a remarkable shade of green that I had curiously never noticed before. I wondered if she'd noticed how much taller I was.

I went back up the hill to our bungalow to learn that we were eating out, as my father had suggested, at Frank & Bob's in South Fallsburg. I don't recall much about that particular meal, other than the fact that my father had franks and beans. I know this because of what occurred after dinner. Starting up the car, he made a quick U-turn, something that summer traffic would render impossible in a few weeks. Almost immediately, he began to make some strange noises. At first, I thought he was just humming, but soon realized it was something far more sinister. My mother said he didn't look too good. Sure enough, my father made a quick right turn just before the railroad tracks and sped toward the now vacant train station. Stopping in a cloud of dust, he desperately ran out of the car and around the back of the building, where his stomach violently rejected Frank & Bob's franks and beans. When he returned to the car, he was visibly pale and shaken. He sat down heavily behind the wheel, leaving the door ajar, letting his head fall back to the top of his seat. My mother told us to roll down the windows to give him plenty of air. She worried about him being able to drive home, but he was the only one there who could. She never learned to drive, and my sister wasn't even fourteen yet. I was two months away from my twelfth birthday, but I said that I was willing to give it a try. My mother just gave me a look. So we waited at the train station for several minutes, my father wiping the sweat from his brow as his color slowly started to return. As he tentatively pulled away, my mother helpfully suggested that he not drive too fast, and that he should avoid any bumps in the road. And to not make any sharp turns. And "I told you not to order franks and beans." My father stared silently ahead, too weak to respond.

Later on, as I climbed into my bed for the first time since last September, I thought that there couldn't be too many feelings better than this. It was the beginning of summer vacation in

The Country. I stretched out on my back under the blanket, just staring up at the ceiling in the darkness, absorbing the sweetness of the moment. No streetlights shone in the window, just a soft glow from the yellow light bulb by our neighbor's front door. My sister was in her bed in the other room listening to Connie Francis singing "Who's Sorry Now?" on the radio. My parents were in the kitchen, my father having his second glass of Alka-Seltzer. It was so quiet. No cars going by on the road, no crickets yet. Our neighbors, the Schultzes, who had arrived a few days earlier, had similarly turned in. It had been a long, eventful day, and I couldn't wait to see what tomorrow would bring.

3

Reunion

Sunday was always a bad day for my father, for it meant he'd
be leaving soon to return to the city. Most fathers, up for the
weekend, wouldn't leave until Sunday night, but not him. It was
a question of beating the traffic, and just getting the departure
over with. Long before lunch, he'd be gone. However, it was
a different story for me. I was settling into a wonderful routine. It turned out to be a cool and mostly sunny week, during
which I went into town a few times to check on the comic book
situation at Fried's, and fishing tackle at Sekofsky's. Sekofsky's
Department Store was one of those places that sold just about
everything. In addition to fishing gear, there were all types
of summer clothing, hardware of every description, assorted
housewares, anything needed for fun in the water, all kinds of
souvenirs like tee shirts and sweats, and lots of aromatic little
cedar boxes marked "Loch Sheldrake, N.Y." The fishing department consisted of a small counter backed by some shelving in
the middle of the store. The clerk was an old man with a hear-
ing aid and glasses who had to be in his eighties. He always
seemed to wear a short-sleeved white shirt, open at the collar,

with suspenders holding up his pants. I thought he might actually be Mr. Sekofsky himself, but of course, never asked. He was not the most pleasant of people, having little patience for customers like me, who mostly looked and rarely bought. This particular visit was not essentially different from the typical pattern. He reluctantly looked up from his newspaper and asked, "What do you want?"

"Nothing. I was just looking."

"What are you looking at?"

"The lures there. The Mepps lures."

"The which?"

"The Mepps lures, the Red Devils," this time much louder.

"Which one do you want?"

In truth, I wanted a lot of them. Mepps lures were considered best for use in local lakes. They were red and white on the front, silver on the back, came in all sizes, and were priced according to size. I didn't actually have money to buy anything.

"Well like I said, I'm just looking."

"Heh?"

"I'm just looking!"

"Then what are you wasting my time for? Go look somewhere else. If you're not buying anything, leave me alone." Which effectively ended this shopping excursion, and I headed back to the colony.

When I wasn't fishing, I would be shooting baskets or playing handball, usually alone, sometimes with someone I didn't know that well, or somebody new. None of my old friends would be coming up until the weekend. I played some pinball and sat on the casino patio with Melanie for a while. In truth, I was occasionally bored. I was almost tempted to complain to my mother that I had "nothing to do," but I knew that would mean huge trouble, and held my tongue.

Friday night meant the return of my father, always a moment much looked forward to by the three of us. He would leave work early in an attempt, often futile, to beat his greatest foe, the traffic, and arrive around dinnertime. My mother would try to time the dinner to be ready shortly after he arrived. When I saw the Mercury turn in the driveway, I ran down to the parking area to greet him.

"Hi Dad! How was the trip?"

"Eh!" This was my father's response to just about all questions which began with "How was . . ." He got out of the car, raising his arms and slowly flapping them up and down, seagull fashion.

"Ahh, it's a *mechiah*. A blessing. It's so hot in that stinking city. That lousy traffic, bumper to bumper all the way back to the Major Deegan. Here, it's so cool. It's delicious. Feel that breeze!"

My father was never hesitant to voice his hatred for the city, and its evil offspring, the traffic. Without question, he loved The Country as much as I did, though perhaps in a different way. He was always a different man at Pesekow's, bearing little resemblance to the moody and often bitter person I knew in the Bronx. He seemed momentarily lost in the mountain air, feeling it caress his arms and breathing deeply. Then, as if remembering I was standing beside him, "So? How's everything, Pops? How's the love life?" he asked, placing his hand on my shoulder. My father called me Pops for the better part of my life, for reasons I'm still trying to figure out.

"Pretty slow. The only girl here is Melanie."

"Melanie, the owners' daughter? Could be worse. So? Is she stacked?"

Not sure how to respond to this, my father's most important question concerning girls, I simply shrugged my shoulders, at the time my favorite response when I didn't know quite what to say. He had a sweat-soaked handkerchief tied around his neck to catch perspiration, and as he turned around, I could see that his shirt back was similarly wet through. I never saw anyone sweat the way he did. As usual, he had several bags of groceries that he brought up from the city, which I grabbed off the back seat and carried as we walked up the hill to the bungalow.

The next morning, Saturday, I saw that there were quite a few more cars around, several with doors and trunks open as people were unloading. My father was arguing with another man about who knew the fastest way to get here and who drove to Pesekow's in the fastest time. As I went by, I only heard my father say, "Two hours from the bridge? You're crazy. Even without traffic . . ." And the other man saying, "I'm telling you, Bernie, I timed it! I was in Loch Sheldrake exactly two hours after I left the bridge." "No way in hell. You better get your watch looked at. It's screwed up," concluded my father, as I continued on my way. I was heading down to the casino to see if I would run into anyone I knew. A couple of teenagers were sitting in a booth, but no one else. I backed out onto the deck before they could give me any trouble. Outside, I looked over the patio railing into the water below, where a few little kids were playing in the shallows with their mothers close at hand. I was watching a few ducks going by farther out in the lake when suddenly, lightning struck.

I heard Melanie's voice calling out, "Philip! Guess who's here!" I turned around to see Melanie coming up the patio steps with none other than Sarah Steinway, my other romantic interest from summers gone by. Here was a vision of overwhelming feminine beauty waving at me as she walked across the deck. I waved back, only to discover that I had been suddenly struck at least partially speechless. I didn't know what to say or how to say it. As I watched her approach, I found myself trying to figure out what there was about Sarah that had changed so much since last year. As she drew closer, it hit me. She was wearing lipstick. Lipstick! My mother wore lipstick, but certainly no twelve-year-old girl I ever knew. Until now. Melanie was giving me one of her elfin girlish grins which clearly meant "Do you see what I see?" Did I ever. I finally managed to get a few words out as we exchanged the usual pleasantries, but I couldn't take my eyes off her lips, and she knew it. If Sarah intended to make a major first impression, she certainly succeeded. I didn't even notice what she was wearing—just the lipstick. I soon realized that I was staring at her face, and not just her lips; her long eyelashes and brown eyes, her long brown hair extending down her back, her smooth skin, her perfect complexion. I don't even know what I said. The girls soon turned away, saying they'd see me later, but all I could do was nod and perhaps mumble "Okay." They both giggled a bit as they stepped off the patio and walked up the path to the bungalows, Sarah looking back over her shoulder at me as they disappeared in the shade under the pines. I had known Sarah for years, but this was the first time I felt nervous in her presence, and I couldn't quite explain it. I worried about whether I remembered to comb my hair that morning, and looked down to see what I was wearing; maybe I should have put on a nicer tee shirt, and not this stupid one with the blue marlin leaping out of the ocean. It was a tee shirt for a little kid, and I vowed right there and then to never wear it again. Cross-currents of uncertain emotions ran through me, and left me wondering what had happened. Something of great importance, no doubt, though what it was and what it meant I didn't exactly know. It left me stunned. What I was pretty certain about, however, was that whatever it was, it meant a heck of a lot more than just lipstick.

The next day turned out to be one of the warmest so far, definitely good for swimming after lunch. Always paying heed to the dictum that one never went swimming right after a meal, I spent some time stretched out on my bed rereading some of my favorite comic books, then went outside. Just across the drive-way from our bungalow was a tiny patch of woods where, deep in the underbrush, I had a secret hideout. It was just a small circle that I had cleared of underbrush, and I loved to crawl in there where no one could see me, but I could view the comings and goings of people as they walked to and from the colony. For me, it was kind of like Superman's Fortress of Solitude, a place where I was able to be alone to think and be private. I had a few such locations stashed around the area that no one knew about, and I cherished their secrecy. I stayed in there for a while, then went down to the casino to check out things in there. All was quiet. Some adults were playing cards on the patio, and some little kids were playing a board game on the floor inside. When I felt that enough time had elapsed, I left the casino intending to go up the hill to the bungalow, but I thought I heard some voices that I recognized coming from the lakeside pier. I went over to the patio railing, and looked down to see not only Melanie and Sarah, but Marty and Ray, my old friends from previous summers, as well! They must have come last night. "Hey Ray! Marty!" I yelled. "Philip!" they yelled back. "When'd you get here?"

"A week ago," I replied, and came down off the patio to see them. "How are you guys doing?" Ray said, "Pretty good," but Marty said, "Good now, but I almost got left back. I had this teacher who hated me. She was about ninety years old, and really mean." "That's terrible," I said. "It's a good thing you didn't flunk." "I know," he said. "It was really close. My mother even went to school to talk to my teacher. That helped a lot, I think."

I asked them what bungalows they were in this year. Ray said Bungalow 3, the same one his family had rented for years. They were known to have the best collection of inner tubes in the colony, all emblazoned with their name in pink nail polish. Marty was in Bungalow 6, directly across from Sarah, in Bungalow 4. "Are you guys going swimming?" I asked. Stupid question, since the four of them were in bathing attire, Ray standing there with a truck-sized inner tube under his arm and nose clips around his neck, Marty with his underwater goggles dangling from his hand. I said I'd go right up to my bungalow to change. As I started to go, Marty yelled, "Well go ahead! We'll wait for you! And hurry up!" "Okay! I'll be right back!" I answered, and took off.

I was thrilled. As with Melanie and Sarah, I had known Marty and Ray ever since we were little kids. It was so good to see them again. Marty was probably my best summer friend. His hair was dark brown, almost black, and, except for a persistent cowlick, hung straight down, though that didn't obscure a face that always seemed to suggest a life far too hard for a kid just turning twelve. Like most kids my age, he was shorter than I was, but a lot stronger. I might even describe Marty as something of a tough guy, with a degree of street smarts I lacked. He never seemed to do well in school, but I did, so together I guess we made a pretty good team. I ran up the hill, my excitement barely in control. Inside the bungalow, my mother was doing some ironing. I ran past her into the bedroom, took off my clothes, and told her that Marty and Ray were here and that I was going swimming. "Oh, that's nice," she said, adding as I left the bungalow in my swim trunks and flip-flops, "Just be careful!" "Okay," I replied as I threw a towel over my shoulder and ran outside, grabbing my inner tube from under the bungalow and proceeding downhill to the lake at a run.

The sidewalk leading down the hill to the pier was at a fairly steep angle, and any kid excitedly running down that hill would pick up some pretty good speed on the way. As I ran down hill, I saw Marty, Ray, Sarah and Melanie waiting for me on the pier, but I never saw the raised crack in the sidewalk that caught my right flip-flop and sent me sprawling. I crashed into the sidewalk and slid several feet, my inner tube flying. All the adults on the pier immediately got up and came running. My friends were horrified. I was in shock. I tried to pick myself up, and looked at my palms, which at first were chalk white, but then turned red with blood. I was bleeding from both knees and had scrapes along both arms. The worst seemed to be a gash in my right ankle that was bleeding terribly. Someone's father got to me first. He looked at my injuries and asked me where my mother was. I told him, and he offered to carry me home, but I couldn't let that happen no matter what. Not in front of my friends. I was so scared and embarrassed. Melanie looked like she was crying. Sarah's hands were over her mouth in horror. Marty and Ray just stared, incredulous. "What bungalow?" I heard the man say. "Nineteen," I replied. "Okay, come on."

We walked slowly up the hill away from the water, through the shade under the pines, then up towards the road and Bungalow 19. When I was within shouting range, I couldn't help but call out, "Ma! Maaaa!" My mother knew that didn't sound good, and came running. "Oh, my God! What happened?" He told her, and I limped into the bungalow and onto my sister's bed. My mother ran cold water on some kitchen towels and proceeded to clean the wounds and try to stop the bleeding.

Mrs. Schultz, who heard all the commotion, came from next door with bandages and an offer to take us to the hospital in Liberty where she felt I could get some stitches for the ankle. My mother saw my frightened reaction to that and said that wouldn't be necessary. At least not yet.

My friends were looking in through the screen door and Mrs. Schultz told them that I'll be fine, I just needed to rest. So they left, saying things like they hoped I'd be feeling better soon, I'd be okay, they'd see me tomorrow, and so on. Sarah stayed a moment longer, looking at me with the saddest eyes, shaking her head, then quickly turned away, saying, "Philip, I'll see you tomorrow, okay?" I just let my head sink back onto the pillow, totally humiliated and in pain from what seemed like fourteen different places. My mother thanked the man who brought me up to the bungalow, and he left. All I remember was Mrs. Schultz and my mother cleaning the injuries with lots of cold water and applying bandages and band-aids all over.

By the next day I was more or less up and around, though limping a bit, sometimes because I had to, sometimes for dramatic effect. It depended on who was watching. My mother had applied copious amounts of mercurochrome to my injuries, whose red color made it look like I was still bleeding, even if I wasn't. The bad news was that my mother said there'd be no swimming until some good hard scabs formed over those cuts and scrapes, especially the ankle, which continued to bleed and ooze for days. That was a blow. It would be a good two weeks with no swimming. Marty had come by to see me around lunchtime, and when I told him about the no swimming, he looked off in thought for a minute, then declared that until I was ready to go swimming again, he wouldn't go in the water either. If I couldn't swim, neither would he. I was shocked and surprised by the gesture. I told him no way, but he meant it. Marty was a rough-edged kid, but I saw now that there was something else there as well, something I had never seen before. What a sacrifice! I didn't know what else to say. Once again, a very significant moment occurred and shook me. There was no lipstick involved this time, but there was a realization that somehow, the

relationships that we had been nurturing for the past few summers had been imperceptibly altered, in a way that would have
full meaning not now, but perhaps at some later point in time.

For a good two weeks I was not able to go swimming, and
Marty stayed true to his word. He did not go in the water once
that entire time. Marty hovered around me like he was some
sort of protector. I thought at times that maybe he thought it
was all his fault, because he was the one who told me to go get
changed and to hurry up. That was ridiculous, of course, but I
thought about it just the same. Sometimes we sat on the patio
watching everyone else in the lake having fun, and feeling good
and sorry for ourselves. Other times we played pinball, cards,
some board games, or went into town. A trip to Sekofsky's fishing counter got us onto the idea of going fishing over at Lake
Evans. Somehow the belief existed that every other lake in the
region had bigger and better fish than Loch Sheldrake. We firmly
believed that Morningside Lake, near Hurleyville, had the best
fishing in the county, but it was about five miles away, and out
of reach. Lake Evans was only about a mile away, and was an
easy walk, even for the walking wounded.

We had gone into Sekofsky's because the last time I was
there I saw these Eagle Claw hooks that came with their own
monofilament leaders, and I wanted to try them out, especially
in Lake Evans. They were forty-nine cents for a three pack, but
I thought they were worth it. The only trouble was that guy
there—the old man. He was so nasty. I was kind of afraid of
him.

"Afraid of that old guy? Are you kidding? He's like a hundred years old. He can barely see," said Marty.

"Yeah, I know. And he's kind of deaf, too. You have to
shout everything."

"Hey look. You want those hooks? Don't worry about it.
Just leave it to me. Come on," Marty said.

I admired his bravado. That teacher he had in sixth grade
must have really loved him. So we went inside the store and

headed right for the fishing counter. I was hoping that maybe today was his day off, but no such luck. He was sitting on a folding chair behind the counter, reading a Jewish newspaper in his lap. Marty looked like he was analyzing the situation, searching for a way to soften the guy up. The man looked up from his newspaper, instantly annoyed, looked at me and said, "Oh. It's you again. Mr. Just Looking."

Before I could respond to the first of what I was sure would be several insults, Marty opened up a new front. "Wow. How can you read that newspaper? There are no vowels."

"Heh?"

"There are no vowels!" yelled Marty, pointing to the newspaper.

"Vowels? What kind of vowels?"

"You know, the dots and stuff underneath the letters that tell you how to pronounce the words. That's the way we read it in Hebrew school, me and my friend."

So that's it, I thought. Let him know that we're Jewish, too. Always a plus. Couldn't hurt.

"Aah, vowels are for kids to read. I don't need vowels. Well? You want something, or what? I'm busy."

Clearing my throat, I said, "I'm interested in those Eagle Claw hooks over there. The three pack? I think I'd like to buy some!" loud enough for half the store to hear. He turned to the Eagle Claw display behind him and handed me the three pack. The price was written in a small circle on the package. He took it back from me, brought it up real close to his eyes, then moved it farther away. Then he took off his glasses completely. He couldn't seem to make out the price.

"Listen," he said to Marty, "what does that look like to you?"

Eager to help out, Marty examined it carefully, and said, "I can see it, mister. It says twenty-nine cents," turning towards me, giving me a secretive wink.

"Heh?"

"I said twenty-nine cents!" Marty yelled. I'm pretty sure people across the street in the barber shop heard that one.

"Is that so? Seems like a bargain. What about you?" he said, handing the hooks back to me. Right away, I could see that I was in a real fix, and started to get pretty nervous. I think he knew the hooks were forty-nine cents all along. If I agreed with Marty, the man would see that we were both liars, and thieves to boot. If I said forty-nine cents, I might be getting Marty in a good bit of trouble for trying to cheat the store. For a moment, I didn't know what to say. The pack certainly read forty-nine cents. I looked at the old man, who was glaring intently at me, his bushy eyebrows twitching above his glasses. I sure did wish I was somewhere else.

"Well? I don't have all day, boy. What do you say?"

Finally, in desperation, I said, "Hey Marty. I think you might need those glasses you were talking about after all. It says forty-nine cents, plain as day."

Without missing a beat, Marty replied "What? No kidding! Let me see that. Hey, you're right! Maybe I should be getting my eyes checked." An acting performance not without merit.

The man, still staring at me, said, "Good for you. That'll be forty-nine cents."

I handed him the two quarters I had in my pocket, and shouted "Thanks a lot!" so he could hear when he returned my penny change. He replied "Any time," smiling just ever so slightly as we walked out of the store.

Outside, Marty complained that he could've gotten the hooks for twenty-nine cents. The old man didn't know which end was up. I disagreed, saying that I thought the guy knew a lot more than we gave him credit for. A whole lot more.

"So what do you think? The guy was faking the whole time just to see what we'd say? Nah, no way," said Marty, and I let it go at that with just a shoulder shrug. We walked back to the colony to get our fishing gear, then left for Lake Evans.

I had at the time an excellent rod and spinning reel, and more fishing tackle than I could possibly use. It all looked and sounded great, though, like when I placed my tackle in my cargo pants pockets in their plastic boxes. I made a wonderful racket when I walked. Marty, on the other hand, used a bamboo pole, no reel, and some green string. I never understood that. He couldn't be poor, spending whole summers at Pesekow's like he did each year. I even had to let him use one of my hooks and a sinker, and replaced his cork float with one of my red-and-white plastic bobbers. So Philip the Fisherman and Huckleberry Finn walked through town and down Route 52 a ways to fish in Lake Evans.

Lake Evans was slightly smaller than Loch Sheldrake and a bit on the weedy side. Both lakes were actually connected by a small stream that drained water from Loch Sheldrake and carried it to Lake Evans. Marty and I once followed that stream to discover where it went. It began alongside Herbie's Restaurant at the end of town, then went underneath Route 52 in a square sided tunnel that you could sort of crawl through on a narrow ledge and hear an echo when you yelled. Traffic going by overhead made a muffled, rumbling sound that we enjoyed because it was so different and otherworldly. Often, if we were around that end of town on a hot day, we'd scramble down the short embankment and edge our way into the tunnel to cool off. It was always cool down there, and the water flow from the lake slowed down to form a pool underneath the road where schools of minnows gathered. Sometimes, we'd take off our sneakers and socks, roll up our pants, and dangle our feet in the water while sitting on the ledge. If we held still long enough, the fish would come over and snoop around our toes. It was kind of a secret place, and we liked the idea that nobody walking by above us had any idea that we were right below their feet.

The strange thing was that sometimes we'd talk about things down there that would not usually turn up in regular conversation. Like the time we were dangling our feet and Marty turned to me and said, "Sarah really likes you, you know. I mean really."

"How do you know?"

"She told Melanie. Melanie told me. Now I'm telling you. They wrote to each other a couple of times over the winter. She probably wants to marry you some day."

"Come on, she's not going to marry me. What are you talking about? That's nuts." The very idea made me kind of scared.

"Oh yeah? She wrote it to Melanie in a letter. I bet her mother is already making arrangements and all. You know, printing up the invitations, reserving a place for the reception, that kind of crap. Don't you know anything? Girls think about that sort of stuff all the time."

"Well I don't. I think it's pretty dumb, if you ask me. Why are you even talking about this? Do *you* ever think about getting married some day? I mean, the person you're going to marry?"

"Nah. Getting married is too far off for me. Right now, I'm worried enough about junior high. I just barely got out of sixth grade, you know."

"Yeah, I remember." Then, after a pause, "Maybe you'll marry Melanie."

Marty just kind of looked at me and smiled a bit at that thought, then we both went back to pondering the minnows in the water.

Anyway, the route we took to go fishing in Lake Evans took us past a farm house that had a working hand-operated water pump in the front yard. We always stopped to pump up some delicious ice cold water. Once at the lake, we baited our hooks with worms we'd dug up the previous day and kept moist and fresh in a dirt-filled coffee can. With my spinning reel, I was able to cast my line far out into the lake. Marty, however, could only cast his line as far as the amount of line he had, which wasn't all that much. It didn't take but fifteen minutes for Marty's bobber to be suddenly pulled under the surface and disappear in the murky water.

He pulled back on the rod, and said it felt like he was stuck on a submerged log. He pulled and pulled, but the hook was stuck tight. We thought for a while that we'd have to cut the line. But then something strange happened. The line began to move. Marty pulled again. That log was alive. Meanwhile, my bobber floated lazily on the surface in the midday sun. Marty, however, was in a major struggle. He was afraid his bamboo pole would break. We set the pole on the ground, and the two of us slowly pulled the line into shore. Fortunately, the string he was using was so thick it could have doubled as clothes line. We soon realized that the log was indeed a fish, and that the fish was huge. Ten minutes of pulling and we finally hauled the fish out of the water and onto the bank. We both stared in shocked disbelief as the fish, not too happy about the whole incident, flopped around in the dirt for a while as he took his final breaths. Marty had caught a sucker, a fish that looked something like a catfish without whiskers. It had a dark brown back, tan sides, and a white belly. It was a true bottom feeder, with a mouth underneath its face, not in front. It had to be three feet long and must have weighed fifteen pounds. We were both screaming with excitement. Marty put the fish back in the water to clean it off, then hoisted it out to begin the walk back home.

Going through Loch Sheldrake village caused a sensation. There was Marty with his bamboo pole, no reel, green string, and the catch of the year. I walked alongside with all my fishing tackle in sheepish silence. People stopped us to ask questions about how it was done, where it was caught, what kind of fish it was, etc. We had stopped in the shade under the Strand's marquee, and within a few minutes a small crowd had gathered around us. Perfect strangers took pictures. The fish turned out to be so big that Marty's mother, who cleaned it and cut its snow white flesh into sections, had enough to feed several colony families. I remember that the cut-up fish filled an entire shelf in his refrigerator. Marty became a hero; the fish, a legend. And I decided to give up fishing, at least for a while.

4

When Frogs Attack

Time eventually worked its magic on my various cuts and scrapes, and my scabs became an object of wonderment for friends and family alike. Marty may have had his fish, but I had my scabs. As far as our celebrity status was concerned, I'd say we were just about equal. Before long, we were both back in the water, and our summertime lives resumed their normal course.

Then there came a cool sunny day, not really fit for swimming, when we decided to head over to the lake's only real swamp, an area known locally as Chinese Alley (why it was so named I have no idea), just to see what we could find. It all sounded innocent enough, but little did we know that our actions over the next hour or two would lead to what came to be known as the Great Frog Festival.

The swamp was on the other side of the lake, and getting there was a matter of walking across the Lakeside Hotel's lawns (the colony's next-door neighbor) and then through about a half mile of woods, eventually coming out in an open picnic area with a covered pavilion, barbeque pit, volleyball court, a rowboat, and the swamp. Chinese Alley was an area of slow-moving water flowing into the lake, and was marked by dead, bleached-silver trees, lily pads, and shocks of tall grass growing up out of the muck. As Marty and I approached the swamp, we were both taken by the amazing number of frogs jumping into the water just ahead of every step we took. They were all fairly small, about two inches, and they were literally everywhere. A few days ago, they were probably about a million black wiggly tadpoles. In a few days, if they ventured into the lake, they would be snack food for the bass and pickerel. As for now, thousands of frogs. We had never seen anything like it. We caught a few, let them go, then caught some more. Then Marty said he had an idea. Back at the pavilion, he remembered seeing a large white plastic bucket overturned on the ground. It would suit our needs perfectly, he said, and ran back to get it. Exactly what our needs were I was about to find out. Marty returned with the bucket and a look on his face that I knew meant trouble.

"Let's catch a whole bunch of frogs, put them in this bucket, and bring them back to the colony," he said.

"What for?" I replied.

"We'll sell them! To little kids! They're too small to go catching frogs by themselves, so we'll bring the frogs to them!"

"Yeah! That sounds great! But how much do we sell them for?"

"I'm not sure."

"Well how about two cents each, three for a nickel. Like pretzels," I suggested, adding, "Two cents isn't that much, even for a little kid. There's always a couple of pennies lying around. They won't even have to ask their mothers!"

Marty agreed. It was a stroke of business acumen rarely seen in two eleven-year-olds. We started the frog harvest right away, but found that it was going too slowly. Another plan needed to be hatched, and it didn't take long. We went over to the picnic area, turned over the rowboat that was stored there, and carried it over to the water, just a few feet away. Marty got in and sat down on the center seat, placing the oars in their fittings. I pushed off from the back, jumping in and onto the back seat, getting only one sneaker wet in the process. Water had poured into my left sneaker as I mistakenly set foot in the lake instead of on dry land as I shoved the boat out into the swamp. It was no problem, as I had done the same maneuver many times before. It was my specialty. After a few strong strokes on the oars, we were in position right where we wanted to be. Marty was a good rower. I got down on my knees without rocking the boat too much, with the bucket right next to me so that I could reach out and grab the frogs from behind and easily place them in captivity.

The frogs were totally out-maneuvered. It seemed like it was only a matter of minutes before the bucket was three quarters full of hysterical jumping and squirming frogs. We put plenty of water in the bucket, added some grass for good measure, and rowed back, leaving the boat just the way we found it. Between the frogs and the water, the bucket was really heavy, so we took turns carrying it as we trekked back to the colony. My left sneaker squished a lot as I walked along, but I didn't care. The Great Frog Festival was almost underway.

No more than ten minutes elapsed between the time we entered the colony and the time that every little kid was running off to get their pennies. There was absolute mayhem, with each kid not wanting to miss out on this great opportunity. Kids soon came running toward us with their pennies from all directions. Some just cupped their hands to carry their purchase away. Others brought water glasses, coffee cups, mixing bowls, and pots of various types and sizes. One kid had what I recognized as a pressure cooker. Some savvy six year olds, knowing a bargain when they saw one, bought six frogs for a dime. Other kids, who could only get a penny, were not turned away empty-handed. There was one kid there who had no money at all, and was staring down into the bucket. He was wearing pretty thick glasses, something you don't tend to see on many little kids, and I felt kind of sorry for him. He looked up at me and said, "I'm pretty sure I could get a penny for you tomorrow. I just don't know where my mother is right now." His eyes were beginning to tear up, and there was no way I was going to let that happen. I reached into the bucket and handed him a frog, which he excitedly enclosed in both hands. "Here you go, kid," I said. "Don't worry about the money. Just be sure to give him a good home." What a look of joy was on his face as he ran off towards his bungalow. Marty was looking at me, and I just said, "What's the difference?" He nodded in agreement. So we made sure that everybody left with at least one frog, no matter what. Many got extras. Before long, though, the customers petered out, and we looked at each other with supreme satisfaction, knowing that we not only made almost three dollars, but that there were now a good number of frogs in every bungalow in Pesekow's. Many, we later learned, soon escaped their confinement and were last seen hopping under beds, into closets, under refrigerators, and so on, then were somehow managing to reappear at the most unfortunate times and places, like the kitchen table during dinner. Looking back on that day, I now realize that it must have been parental hell. But no matter. Business is business. We still had some frogs left in the bucket, so we went down to the lake behind the handball court and let them go in the water. We stood there watching them joyously swim off in all directions, happy to have their freedom back. Marty and I shook hands on a job well done. Our work for the day was finished.

It took quite a number of days for the frog mayhem to settle down, but before long, Pesekow's was once more at peace, and our pictures were no longer on display in the Loch Sheldrake post office. Feeling confident that we could once again come out during daylight hours, Marty and I one morning were skipping stones out behind the handball court, one of our favorite hangouts. A cloudy-bright sky and calm winds left the lake with barely a ripple, perfect for skipping stones across its surface. This was something I really liked to do, especially competitively, because I had a really good arm, and could beat just about everyone, even teenagers, which is probably one of the reasons this particularly nasty teenager, Mitchell Black, was always after me. One time, Marty and I were just watching, and Mitchell skipped a stone eleven times, which is pretty good. He dared anyone watching to beat him. No one could. Except me. At least I was pretty sure I could. I searched the shallows for a while, and eventually found the perfect stone—not too light, not too heavy, sort of round of course, and pretty flat, though not too flat. After several back and forth arm motions, the rock cradled between my thumb and forefinger, I was just at the right angle to the water, and sent my rock sailing. It skipped fourteen times. Mitchell's buddies hollered and hooted, and he turned kind of red. That was our signal to leave, so the two of us got out of there fast, before the next stone went flying in our direction.

Today, however, our interest had begun to wane, so we decided to shoot some baskets instead. Marty said he'd wait at the basketball court while I went up to my bungalow to get the ball. I wanted to get a drink of lemonade from the fridge anyway; it was pretty warm out. But as soon as I pulled the screen door open and stepped inside, I knew that something was very wrong. The door to the bathroom was closed, and I could hear my mother yelling at my sister to calm down inside. I knocked on the door and asked "What's the matter?"

My mother immediately answered "Philip! I'm so glad you're here. Go in the kitchen and wait there. I'll be right out." Which she was, sweating a bit, her hair in atypical disarray. She wrote something on a piece of paper, and handed it to me along with a dollar bill. "Look. I need you to go right into town, to Fried's. Give this to the pharmacist in the back of the store, and bring what he gives you right back here. Right away, you hear?"

"What's going on with Sheila?"

"Never mind. Just get going."

I knew the tone of urgency when I heard it, so without delay, I stuffed both the note and the dollar in my pocket and headed for town. I hadn't been walking a minute when I heard Marty's voice calling from behind me. He wanted me to wait for him, but I told him I couldn't. Running, he caught up to me in a few seconds.

"What's the matter? I thought we were going to shoot baskets."

"I can't. Something's wrong with my sister, and I have to go to Fried's to get something for her."

"What is she, sick?"

"I don't know."

"Well what do you have to get?"

"I said I don't know. My mother wrote it on a note."

"Let's see."

This was typical of Marty. Virtually everything that happened anywhere in his vicinity was his business. I didn't really see the harm, so I handed him the folded note as we swiftly walked into the village.

"Oh wow," he said, reading the contents. "Kotex."

"Kotex? What's Kotex? Some kind of medicine?"

"Jeez, Philip. Sometimes I think you don't know anything. Don't you know that girls have to have Kotex when they get their periods? You do know what a period is, don't you?"

"Of course I do. I'm not dumb, you know." Actually, I had no idea. My reluctance to admit to someone that I didn't know or understand something is what would lead me, several years down the road, to a number of disastrous encounters with high school mathematics. The teacher, who could spot the look of total befuddlement a mile away, would call on me and say, "You understand that, Philip? Any questions?"

"Oh, no, Mrs. Perretti, no questions. I'm all set." When in fact, I was completely clueless.

"So you know about periods?"

"Sure I do. I have a sister, you know." All I could imagine was tiny black dots covering my sister's face, like measles; a bad case of periods. My only hope was that the pharmacist, when I handed him the note, would provide some sort of directions about the medicine being purchased, as they often do. "Oh, yes, of course," I would smugly say, adroitly concealing how deep in the dark I actually was.

Marty decided to wait outside Fried's. Maybe he, like the math teachers waiting for me in the future, detected the truth, and didn't want to be tainted by my ignorance. Inside, a few teenagers were banging away at the pinball machines by the window and a couple of kids I didn't know were looking through the comic books stacked in a rack nearby. Some people were at the soda fountain, others browsing through the narrow aisles under the store's glaring flourescent lights. The pharmacy was at the back of the store, and thankfully wasn't busy, although I had to cough a few times to get the druggist's attention, who, with a hand gesture, asked me to wait a moment. It looked like he was counting pills into one of those little pill bottles. He finally came over, glanced at my note, quickly retrieved a large blue box from a shelf against the wall, and brought it to where I was standing next to the cash register. One furtive glance at the box revealed three words in plain white lettering: "Kotex Sanitary Napkins."

Napkins! Holy Cow, I thought. What does she want with a box of napkins? My mother usually placed an open box of napkins on the kitchen table, but I never saw this particular brand before. I just don't get it, I thought, staring at the box, more confused than ever. The pharmacist, meanwhile, rang up the sale, placed the box in a bag, and asked, "Any questions?"

And there it was. This moment, to be repeated many times in my lifetime, would eventually become my own personal moment of truth. Little did I know it then, but I was laying the foundation for years of befuddling misery when I promptly responded, "Oh, no, mister. No questions. I'm all set."

Outside, a big tractor trailer truck went rumbling noisily down the street as I found Marty sitting on a car's fender outside the store. He had a mouthful of bubble gum, and was reading the little comic strip found inside the gum wrapper, detailing the further adventures of Bazooka Joe. He wanted to know how everything went inside, and I responded with all the complacency I could muster that I was, indeed, "All set." He also wanted to have a close-up look at the box in the bag, but I decided to refuse. I'm not sure why. Maybe I was protecting my sister's privacy. Maybe I was just being obstinate. In any case, it seemed like a good idea at the time.

"Come on, let me see the box!"

"Why? What's the matter? You never saw a Kotex box before?"

"Sure I have. Lots of times. I just wanted to see this one."

"What's the big deal? They're all the same. Don't you know that?"

"I know, I know. I just . . . well, never mind. Forget it." He seemed pretty sore, kind of revealing to me that maybe he didn't know quite as much as he let on. I felt I had him, at least for the moment. We walked back to Bungalow 19 in silence, both of us more or less acknowledging that a stand-off had taken place. I handed my mother the bag, retrieved my basketball from under the bed, and got out of there fast. My sister was still in the bathroom. I didn't want to know why. Bouncing the ball between us as we went downhill, it seemed that a strategic decision was made to just leave certain subject areas undiscussed any further, at least for the time being, which was all right by me. Arriving at the basketball court, we retreated to ground far more familiar to us, and decided to play a game of Horse until it was time for lunch.

5

Entertainment

When evening came to Pesekow's Bungalow Colony, it generally found us pursuing one of a handful of activities. One was going to the movies. The Strand would get its films from the Rivoli in South Fallsburg, which in turn, got its films from Monticello. "Tammy and the Bachelor," a leftover from the previous summer, was not high on the list of movies we absolutely had to see, but the girls wanted to go, and since we were of late a couple of rich businessmen, we agreed to take them. This particular summer found me attaching myself to Sarah, though in the past, exclusivity was certainly not part of any arrangement. This year seemed to be different, though. Maybe it was the lipstick, which, by the way, was never seen again after that first fateful encounter on the patio. Maybe once was enough. Marty, for now, was paired up with Melanie.

My mother was aware that I was spending way more time than usual in the bathroom lately, combing and recombing my hair, and tonight was no exception. I wasn't satisfied until each and every hair was in its exact intended place, and only when that occurred did I put the comb down, pleased with how I

45

looked. I even secretly (so I thought) used some of my sister's hair spray to stiffen things up so that no errant breeze could move a single hair out of place. Ever since that day on the patio, I had been combing my hair at least twice a day, and even began to occasionally wash my hands. This was a level of personal grooming and a vague awareness of hygiene that my mother hadn't quite seen in me before. It was a change that did not go unnoticed.

"Where're you going?"

"Who, me? Uh, just to the movies," very nonchalant.

"With Sarah?"

"Yeah, and Marty and Melanie too."

"Don't worry. You look fine."

"Huh? What do you mean?" I asked, shrugging my shoulders like I had no idea what she was referring to.

"You know. You look fine."

A shoulder shrug worked so often in place of a verbal response that I tried it again, and went for the door.

"Don't be too late."

"I won't"

"You need money?"

"Nah, I'm fine."

"Enjoy the movie," she said, and I responded, "I will. Bye." Somehow, I just didn't want to be questioned any further about my appearance or anything relating to a relationship between me and Sarah. I was glad to be out of the bungalow, and headed down hill to meet my friends.

Once the summer season shifted into high gear, usually around the last week in June, the theatre had two showings nightly. We always went to the early show, as we did this night. The Strand had a ticket booth right out front with a small sign that read ADMISSION .50—and, beneath that, UNDER 12, .35. I sometimes had trouble paying the kid's price because I was so tall, especially if the person in the booth was a teenager and didn't know any better, but not tonight. Once inside, our first stop was the snack counter for popcorn and candy; then we entered the theatre itself and made ourselves comfortable in four red velvet seats near the back.

After coming attractions (*Gigi*), and the Merry Melodies cartoon (Bugs Bunny and Elmer Fudd), *Tammy* came on screen, with Debbie Reynolds singing her lilting love song. It had its desired effect. Both Marty and I were madly in love with Debbie Reynolds before half the movie was over. The immediate effect on us though, was to provide us with the emotional confidence to place our arms around the shoulders of our girls. This was always a suspenseful moment, but tonight our efforts were rewarded with not only no resistance, but with what might have been a little encouragement as well.

When the movie was over, tradition had us stopping by Fried's for ice cream sodas, a malted, or the like. Fried's soda fountain lined one entire side of the store, having a dozen or so chrome stools with revolving red vinyl seats. We ordered our refreshments, the girls talking about how handsome Leslie Nielsen was, Marty and I countering with the wonders of Debbie Reynolds. Then it was a slow walk back to the colony, preferably holding hands. Tonight, we happened to find our way down to the casino. A few adults were sitting out on the patio, which was lit by a single spotlight over the door. Inside, some teenagers were at the pinball machine, the jukebox playing Danny and the Juniors' "At the Hop" in the background. We decided to take a look around the back of the casino, as it was called, to see if it was currently occupied. Once our eyes became accustomed to the darkness, we saw that there was no one there. The highly coveted romantic spot was currently ours.

The casino had one window facing the back, and tonight it allowed no more than a few feeble rays from inside to shine onto the deck. But in the far corner, darkness reigned supreme. We occupied a wooden bench facing the water. The lake was absolutely black, and the illuminated windows and outside lights of the houses and cottages spread out on the opposite shore were reflected across the water in long lines of liquid light. Stars filled the sky from horizon to horizon, a source of wonderment for a group of city kids, who could never behold such a sight back home. Occasionally, there'd be the sound of a distant airplane, its location made evident by a slowly moving dot of light across the heavens. Inside the casino, we could hear The Platters singing "Twilight Time." Sarah started swaying just a bit to the music, turned to me and said, "Let's dance, okay?" "Here?" I said, adding "Now?" "Yeah," she said, similarly adding "Now. Please?" So with Marty and Melanie looking on in the darkness, Sarah and I slowly danced to "Twilight Time." It was hardly a dance. We just kind of held each other, moving around the dark deck a little bit. Sarah rested her head against my shoulder, and I held her pretty close. It was nothing short of wonderful. The music inside the casino soon stopped, but before sitting back down, Sarah looked up at me in a way I had never seen before, and have seldom seen since. We kissed. It wasn't the first time, nor was it to be the last, but it was certainly different. Returning to the bench, Melanie's bright smile revealed her understanding that something was afoot between Sarah and me. Marty, ever the sophisticate, said, "What's with you two?" I said, "Nothing," shrugging my shoulders feigning ignorance, and looked back out over the water. A slight breeze off the lake resulted in a comment by Melanie that it was chilly back there tonight, which was all we needed to edge just a little bit closer. Some hands held, some arms around the shoulders, and a few added soft kisses made the evening blissfully complete.

On weekends, the Lakeside Hotel, just up the road, would have a live band playing in the Gold Room, their entertainment venue. It was strictly for hotel guests, but that never stopped us. This sort of an evening called for dressing up, which for me meant a shower and a higher level of clothes than jeans and a tee shirt. I didn't want to be a show-off, but I certainly wanted to impress Sarah tonight with my attire. After all, there was a fine line between dressing up and dressing over the top, so I had to be careful. With that in mind, I made the decision to wear my genuine cowboy belt with the silver buckle shaped like a horseshoe. Standing before the bedroom mirror, I saw that it was the perfect complement to my sport shirt and slacks. Just the right touch. I edged the back of my shirt collar up a bit, but not too much—I didn't want to look too "rocky." Glancing left and right, up and down, all was in place. Sarah couldn't help but be overwhelmed.

We usually met right outside Melanie's house, which was up by the road, adjacent to the second driveway. It was the only year-round, private residence on the premises. Strangely enough, we were never invited in. Melanie always met us in the driveway, coming out through the garage. And they had a television, too, thanks to a huge antenna on the roof. We didn't mention it much; never in Melanie's presence. There was just this distance that the Pesekows always maintained between the owners and the renters. They were always friendly, never friends. Melanie, of course, maintained no such distance, but no doubt had rules to comply with. Besides, we didn't care about the TV. In The Country, TV simply ceased to exist. In any case, Marty and the girls were waiting when I got there. The girls, as always, rose to the occasion by wearing a pretty dress, appropriately held aloft by layers of crinoline underneath. They looked terrific. Marty was all cleaned up in a sport shirt and slacks like mine, though I thought he could've changed his sneakers. It was a matter of only a few minutes to walk to the hotel, just up the road.

Somehow, we never entered the Gold Room without several guests commenting about how "cute" we were, and what "adorable" couples we made. Maybe because the average Lakeside guest was about seventy-five. Or maybe it could have been that we really were cute. We had no way of knowing.

The Gold Room was in a separate building to the right of the hotel. Inside was a fairly large room with a stage at one end and a refreshment stand at the other. Many chairs were arranged along the walls, and tables adjoined the refreshment area. On stage was usually a five-piece band—piano, drums, saxophone, trumpet or clarinet, and vocalist, who sometimes also played an instrument, like a guitar or accordion. The music was already playing when we got there, so we walked right in and moved onto the dance floor amid a good-sized crowd of hotel guests.

Dancing was a major part of our social lives then. The girls were always teaching us the latest dances and the latest moves. Somehow, they always knew. We never did. Latin music and the cha-cha were very big that summer, so it was no surprise that the band next played "Cherry Pink and Apple Blossom White," followed after a while by the "Tea for Two Cha-Cha." Any dance that even had the slightest chance of getting anyone winded was always followed by something slower so that the guests could recover their breath. They didn't want any medical emergencies on the dance floor. So "Volare" was next, which accomplished that purpose. After every few songs or so, the band leader, who often doubled as a vocalist and comedian, would talk to the crowd, and tell a few bad jokes (often involving the management and owners of the hotel, who were always present), all in good fun. Some of the jokes we just didn't get. That was our signal to buy some sodas and take a break ourselves, sitting a few out to watch the people dance and to tell a few private jokes of our own. Sometimes we'd step out onto the porch and watch the comings and goings in front of the Gold Room. We never stayed late, so after an hour or so we'd walk up the hill to the road and head back. There was an old stone wall that curved along part of the driveway and paralleled the road. The girls, just for fun, jumped up onto the wall and walked along its top, with us holding their hands to keep them steady. The wall ended at the colony's property line, and each girl turned toward us to be helped down. I held Sarah's waist and eased her down off the wall, as did Marty for Melanie. I'll never forget that. I thought that was the most romantically mature thing we had ever done. The thank you kiss on the cheek was absolutely terrific. Walking back along the road, one couldn't help but think that life couldn't get much better.

More often than not, we'd gravitate toward the casino on a given evening, especially if it was raining. A lot of dancing went on there as well. The jukebox played 78s and was well stocked with a combination of current rock-and-roll hits, dance tunes, and golden oldies. A quarter played five records. Some nights it seemed as though the whole bungalow colony was there. Lots of adults would be playing cards in the next room, which was very brightly lit and always filled with lots of cigarette smoke. In the casino itself, we'd be dancing or just hanging out. Little kids liked to watch the bubbles rising through the yellow tubes on the front of the jukebox. If we had enough people, we'd be sure to play "The Stroll," by the Diamonds, with two parallel lines of dancers "strolling" through the room. Once, the teenagers, who were usually our bitter enemies, called a temporary truce so that we could all join forces and have enough people to "stroll across the floor."

Peaceful coexistence with the teenagers also occurred, if conditions were right, in the back of the casino, where scary stories were told. It was there, for example, that I first learned the terrifying truth about the monster living in the depths of the lake, the creature known only as Krepsi. Somehow, the teenagers felt it was their responsibility and obligation to teach us about certain subject areas in which they were experts, like the real meaning of a few choice four-letter words, what women really want, and of course, Krepsi. As the story was told, no one had actually ever seen Krepsi and lived to tell about it. But the legend persisted, probably having its foundation in the notion that Loch Sheldrake itself was known, at least among the kids, as a body of water of unknown depth. There was this one teenager named Mel, who despite the fact that he hung around with a bunch of young gangsters in training, was a terrific storyteller. So the story would once again be told, with a group of us sitting in rapt attention in the darkness of the back of the casino on a particularly appropriate night: ". . . and the lake is so deep that no one knows for sure what's actually down there. They've run tests. They've never hit bottom! But this much is known. On certain dark nights, especially during the first week of July [or whatever week it happened to be], Krepsi comes out of the depths and crawls onto the land looking for victims to eat. Its appetite is incredible. It can eat two, three kids a night, if it's really hungry. That's why the Pesekows built that fence along the shore line. Did you happen to see it? It's to help keep Krepsi out. So they think. It loves young kids the best. You know why? They're still soft and juicy. Remember that kid who was here last year, Charlie something? Did you notice that he's not back this year? You know why? Krepsi got him! Last year, July 2nd. What? That's tonight?" And so on. If the story was told with enough embellishments, it really got the girls going, and if there were younger kids present, they might actually run off crying. And if the truth were known, I may have looked over my shoulder a few extra times as I walked back home in the night. Maybe.

Sometimes we'd be sucked into the casino's major vice, the pinball machine. There were actually two, but one was really popular. And incredibly addictive. It was a horse racing game. When you inserted your nickel, the game came alive with ringing bells and flashing lights, choosing at random which horse in a field of nine would be yours for this particular race. As you pulled back the plunger and sent your silver ball up the chute into the game itself, it was your job to hit as many of your horse's bumpers as possible to get your horse to win. Each bumper hit sent your horse moving forward. If your horse happened to come in first, you won a free game. Sometimes five free games, sometimes fifty, depending on the horse, the odds, track conditions, etc. A fifty game winner always had a crowd of admirers around him, as if it was the high stakes poker table at Monte Carlo. Games would be given out to favorites in the crowd. It often would take an entire evening to play down the fifty games. Not that it happened that often. More than once, Mr. Pesekow had to pull the plug on the machine at ten o'clock or so to get everyone to get out and go home. Amid groans of protest, we'd all reluctantly leave, ever so slowly, to try our luck another day.

Sometimes, money became an issue. Playing pinball cost a nickel a game, the jukebox a quarter, movies thirty-five cents a person in the evening. Going out on a date could easily top a dollar. That was real money, and we couldn't count on a Great Frog Festival more than once a summer. Both Marty and I were on many a parent's hit list over that event. So when all else failed, we got down on our hands and knees and crawled into the cool darkness underneath the casino's patio to look for money. The decking making up the patio's floor had pretty wide spaces in between the boards. Gin rummy, poker, mah-jong, and such were usually played for money, and coins were always falling off the tables onto the floor, often slipping through the cracks and disappearing below. That's where we came in. If we were lucky enough to be under there when it hadn't been mined in a while, we sometimes would find a good handful of nickels, dimes, and the occasional quarter. But it wasn't without its perils. In addition to just getting filthy, never a real problem for any of us, or encountering beetles and spiders of all shapes and sizes, there was the time that my young friend Mark, from the basketball court, was creeping around down there doing some mining of his own and came across Stan, the colony's handyman, sleeping one off. He thought Stan was dead. That was the last time Mark crawled under the patio looking for anything, and it was warning enough for the rest of us.

During those times when money was scarce, and there was still a while to go to the next allowance, we would sometimes walk up the road to the Overlook, a small hotel complex opposite the Lakeside, to catch a movie in their rec hall, as they called it. The movies were free for guests; once again, we'd all just walk in like we belonged there, and as a result, there was never a problem. A 16mm projector was set up in the back of the room, and a screen lowered from the ceiling directly in front of a small stage. The place looked a little like my school's auditorium, only much smaller.

On one particular night, the movie was called *Song Without End*, and was about Frederick Chopin, the composer. None of us had ever heard of him, or the movie for that matter, but it was in color, and free, so we went. Marty was with Melanie, and I went with Sarah, as usual. The movie at first was pretty boring, and consequently, we started whispering and giggling to each other, and were yelled at by a woman sitting in front of us. Marty wanted to throw some M&Ms he was eating at the screen, but we told him that wouldn't be right, and the ammunition reverted back to food.

Things changed, at least for me, about halfway through the film. I had never heard "Polonaise" before, and I stared at the screen and became totally immersed in the music. I had never heard anything so wonderful, so moving, so lyrical, in my life. I tried memorizing the predominant melodies so that I could play it over and over in my mind when it wasn't being played on screen. "Polonaise" left me in a state of amazement that anyone could write music that was so beautiful. I wished I had it on a record back home so that I could play it on the hi-fi. Maybe I could save up and buy it at the record store back in the Bronx. At the end of the film, a close-up of Chopin's hands playing the piano showed his hands slowly withdrawing from the keyboard. The music stopped, then returned when "The End" came on screen. The lights came back on, and we went out into the night.

As we headed back to the colony, we talked about whether that ending meant he had died, or simply stopped playing. I wanted to believe that he simply stopped playing, and that he went on to write a lot more music, but I reluctantly realized that it must have signified his death. The world of classical music had been a totally alien environment for me, but no longer. That evening, watching *Song Without End* at the Overlook Hotel, gave me a brief glimpse into a wonderful world of music that I would revisit again and again for the rest of my life. The girls and Marty were joking about the film, making sarcastic comments about this or that particular scene, but I was in another world entirely, playing "Polonaise" over and over in my mind as we walked back home along the road.

Of course, the recreational and activity center for just about everyone at the colony was the lake. Our swimming area was in a little cove, with the casino and its patio extending almost to the water's edge on the left, and some woods on the right. On any given sunny afternoon, the pier and grassy slope surrounding it would be covered with blankets, lawn chairs, towels thrown everywhere, and car and truck inner tubes of various sizes for use in the water. We all had our own inner tubes, and we'd use them according to our particular whim—as life preservers, as private water craft, or as something to simply hold on to when out "over our heads."

Barry, our life guard, occupied a spot in a rowboat in deep water. That boat was the absolute boundary beyond which no one was allowed to go. Not that we tried. None of us wanted to hear Barry's whistle being blown in our direction because we had ventured out too far. So we spent our time diving to the bottom with goggles (which always leaked) covering our eyes, nose clips firmly attached to what were often slippery nostrils, or paddling around in our inner tubes, just having watery fun.

Parents rarely touched the water. Sometimes, if the sun became a bit too much to bear, somebody's mother would announce that she was going to "take a dip"—an immersion that would last no longer than two minutes or so—and would be looked upon with wonder and admiration by the other parents present. As far as we were concerned, we didn't leave the water until ordered to do so, purple lips and wrinkled fingers being the clue that it was time to take a break.

The only thing we really wanted but didn't have in the water was a raft—a floating platform that we could swim out to, dive off of, or just sit upon. There was only one other bungalow colony on the lake, and it was over on the other side, directly across from us. Lowenthal's Colony was smaller than Pesekow's, but they had the luxury of a terrific raft, anchored about fifty feet off shore, and we would often look out across the water with an insulted envy that bordered on raging jealousy. We sometimes heard the teenagers discussing semi-secret plans to row over there and steal it in the night, then tow it across the lake to our side, a spoil of undeclared warfare with Lowenthal's. But much to our displeasure and disappointment, nothing ever came of it, the raft persisting across a half mile of open water, an unattainable prize beyond our reach.

The woods adjacent to the swimming area covered several acres, and had a lakeside trail that led to Max's boathouse, where one could rent motorboats or rowboats, learn to water ski, have a snack, or play the omnipresent pinball machines. Along the trail, about halfway through the woods, was a large, concrete rectangular block in a small clearing. It had to be about six feet long, some three feet wide and deep. It must have weighed many tons, and had no markings on it whatsoever. Although we often called it the Big Rock, it was no rock—it was made of cement, its purpose, and how it got there, a total mystery. We loved it, and would sometimes go there, sit down on it, and talk about how it got there, who put it there, when, and more importantly, why. Many of the theories we discussed were supernatural, and always succeeded in adding to the block's mysterious origins. Some of our theories tied the block to the well-known association between Loch Sheldrake and The Mob. There were always stories circulating about mobsters coming up from the city to dump a body or two into the lake's shadowy depths. That led to the notion that the block itself just might be the final resting place of some poor gangster who suffered a grisly fate at the hands of Murder Inc. Often, just to create the proper atmosphere, we'd remind ourselves that those very woods stood on the former site of a place called the Loch Sheldrake Casino, a gambling den of such notoriety that the local police were reluctant to go near the place. So we tended to think a lot about who or what just might be inside the mysterious block. Needless to say, we never went there at night.

Speaking of mysteries, a little further along the trail, just before getting to the boathouse, was a small dock to which two vintage motorboats were tied. They were never rented, never used. No motors were attached. They were both made of wood, in perfect condition, and were streamlined beauties from another time. One was named Gorgeous Gus, the other, Candy. Gorgeous Gus was varnished wood, shiny and highly polished. Candy was painted white, with green trim. Their plush interiors showed no sign of human occupation. In rainy weather, they were covered with form fitting tarps to protect them from the elements; when the weather turned fair, the tarps would be gone, and there they'd be in their perfectly preserved splendor.

The rumor about these boats, and we loved to hear and then retell this story almost as much as the tales about Krepsi, was that there once was a grand race many years ago, Gorgeous Gus versus Candy for ultimate lake supremacy. It was to be once around the lake's perimeter, with hundreds of people lining the shore in town to witness the historic event. There was the firing of the starter's gun, and both boats roared away, turning the water wild in their wakes. They both sped along the shore, with neither taking a decisive lead. Then, somewhere out on the far side of the lake, something happened. The boats could barely be seen, but there was no doubt that they were no longer moving. People wondered, and strained their eyes to see. Some people thought they heard gunfire; others swore they saw something in the water, just in front of the racing boats. In any case, a speedboat soon left town, heading across the water to where the boats were stopped. After what seemed like an eternity on the other side of the lake, it soon became apparent that Gorgeous Gus and Candy were slowly being towed back to town. So the race was sadly never finished, having ended in a cloud of mystery somewhere out on the water, far from the finish line. Exactly what it was that stopped the race remained open to speculation and our eager imaginations, its details existing in that blurry area where fact, over time, becomes fused with fancy. Nevertheless, the boats were never raced, or even used, ever again. And there they sat, as they had on the day of their great race, waiting for riders who would never be coming.

My mother Millie, my sister Sheila and I (giving the "okay" sign with my hand) next to the Mercury, taken at the scenic overlook at the dreaded Route 17 hairpin turn at the top of the Bloomingburg hill; on the way to Pesekow's, June 1957.

Same trio, same location, with Sullivan County in the distance. Note that a lengthy trip by car required considerable dressing up in the '50s.

Having arrived at Pesekow's, my father Bernie leans against the Mercury. Some bungalows are in the background, as is a glimpse of the lake and the casino patio in the upper left.

My father, in his traveling attire, poses in the driver's seat of his beloved '57 Mercury, a car which ironically gave him no end of mechanical trouble.

My mother, sister and I pose on the picnic table in front of Bungalow 19 on what was known as "the hill", location of the colony's three single family bungalows. My mother, but not my sister, has changed into more comfortable clothing, having worked to set up the bungalow for the summer ahead.

The author strikes a pose, same location. This, and the previous photos, were taken in early June, 1957, driving to, and arriving at Pesekow's.

My sister Sheila, hands on hips, white blouse, taken outside our bungalow. 1956

My mother and father together in a lounge chair with their friend and neighbor "Arnie Schultz" leaning on the chair's back; lots of smiles. Behind are some of the bungalows that housed multiple families. 1956

My father in a lounge chair (wearing as a prank his goofy glasses), my sister with her arm around his shoulder. My father became a different person in the country, shedding his more somber Bronx personality for a much lighter one, as seen here. 1956

My father lounges in the grass adjacent to the lake. Part of the pier can be seen in the background. 1956

Right: My mother sitting on the pier, with her feet in the water, typical of parents, who rarely swam, though my mother was an excellent swimmer. Our lifeguard, "Barry," is in the rowboat. 1956

Below: In the lake. I'm on the right, my arms outside the inner tube, my sister (checkered swimsuit) behind me, her friend and brother next to us. On the left, swimming toward us, is my best friend, "Marty." 1956

In the lake. The author is in the inner tube in the foreground, my friend "Marty" looking on (in white tee shirt) disapprovingly. Some additional kids and teens (and some parents!) in the background, with ever-present inner tubes. Families often came to be known by the quality of their inner tubes, usually marked with pink or red nail polish. 1956

My parents, Bernie and Millie Ratzer, standing near the lake, in what undoubtedly was their best of times. 1956

My father poses on "Bart Sheridan's" famous motorcycle. He and Bart developed a friendship that lasted some twenty years, far beyond Pesekow's. 1958

My father, in motorcycle cap, poses with the author (flannel shirt) on the casino patio. 1958

My mother and visiting grandmother pose with the author (kneeling on top of the table) at the picnic table by Bungalow 19. I am wearing the leaping marlin tee shirt I describe in the book as something a younger kid would wear and vow never to wear again after my meeting with Sarah Steinway. 1958

6

Cast & Crew

Populating the colony was an interesting cast of characters, who every now and then provided their own sort of entertainment for whatever audience happened to be gathered around. An example of this might be the time that Monica Black, mother of Mitchell Black, teenager gone bad, started parading around the colony wearing her underwear as outerwear. I'll never forget the time I was hanging around the pier with my buddies and she came walking down the sidewalk. She was kind of tall, with short red hair, a style my mother once referred to as a pageboy, though I can tell you Mrs. Black looked nothing like a boy. She was wearing a black bra and panties. And flip-flops. Nothing else, unless you count earrings. Everybody stared, amazed, at the display. She, however, was completely carefree and unconcerned, less self-conscious than a two-year-old. I stared in disbelief, finding this to be very interesting. She had her pack of Pall-Malls and a book of matches stuck into her bra. After all, she had no pockets. She was carrying a folded lounge chair, which she opened up and stretched out upon to relax in the sun. Women playing mah-jong up on the deck stopped in midplay, their tiles momentarily silent. Old Mr. Bloom, who always sat reading in a chair with his feet in the water, stopped reading entirely, closing his book for an unusually long time. His bookmark fell into the water and floated away, but he didn't seem to notice, or care. Of note is the fact that it was midweek, meaning that most men, her husband included, were away until the weekend. The only men present in the colony were a few retirees like Mr. Bloom, one or two husbands on vacation, and an occasional delivery man. So no doubt Mrs. Black felt that such attire (or lack of it) was fitting and proper for whatever she had in mind. If this had occurred once, it might have been attributed to sun stroke, or some sort of mental instability. But such was not the case. This became her regular lakeside attire, and our regular lakeside entertainment, for quite some time. Besides, everyone knew that Mrs. Black was about as mentally unstable as a hungry shark.

As if her underwear wasn't enough of a scandal, we had all heard the story of how Mrs. Black was accused by Mrs. Stern of fooling around with her husband. This happened in the casino card-room one night. There were lots of people present who saw and heard the whole thing, and were more than anxious to let everyone in the colony know the details. Mrs. Black didn't deny anything. Instead, she said something like, "Oh yeah? What are you going to do about it?" So Mrs. Stern slapped her across the face. Mrs. Black, not to be outdone, reached back and wallopped Mrs. Stern so hard she fell backwards onto the floor. Mrs. Black stood over her and said, "What else are you going to do?" There was a lot of cursing in both directions, but no more punches thrown. People soon separated the two women, Mrs. Stern in tears and Mrs. Black gloating. A couple of women took Mrs. Stern back to her bungalow. After that incident, Mr. Stern, who wasn't in the card room that night, stopped coming up on weekends. Then one day Mrs. Stern hired a car from Mendel's Taxi Service and left for the city. She never returned. As one might expect, no one complained to Mrs. Black about her underwear, and everyone wondered what became of the Sterns.

A word about Mitchell Black, Monica's son, and what characterized his having "gone bad." Mitchell was a bastard. I don't mean that literally, but then again, who knows? However, in a figurative sense, he was the meanest, most hateful person I had ever known. He had a crew cut, and was overly fond of muscle shirts, probably because he was a weight lifter, and proud of his physique. He was the kind of kid mothers tended to call a bully. For one reason or another, he and I were always crossing paths, though I tried to keep my distance. Maybe I was an easy target, being so much younger, but really tall and thin. I wasn't exactly sure why, but he never let an opportunity to annoy me pass him by. Mitchell was sixteen, and smoked as much as his mother. He seemed to take endless delight in belittling, irritating, and making miserable those he could push around. For example, he once took my basketball from me while I was shooting hoops, and wouldn't give it back. Finally, when I started up the hill to my bungalow to tell my mother, he threw the ball at me with such force that it almost knocked me down. From a safe distance, I told him to go do something to himself that I knew was an awful thing to say, and he came after me; but outrunning Mitchell was no problem; he gave up after a brief chase. Victorious, I yelled out, "You'll get yours," an expression I'd heard Jackie Gleason say to his wife on *The Honeymooners,* and ran off.

Mitchell did indeed get his shortly thereafter. He had a girlfriend from another colony named Kathleen, who everyone described as a tramp. I never understood that, since she looked nothing like my idea of a hobo. But one night, he took Kathleen out on a date in his mother's car. Unfortunately, he didn't have a license. He got in a minor accident and left the scene. It took the state police about one day to track him down to the colony. Seeing Mitchell being taken away by the police for questioning was one of the most joyous experiences of the summer. I was standing by the driveway with my friends when the police car drove by, Mitchell in the back seat. We all pointed at him and laughed uproariously. We even started singing an impromptu song, "We Love to See You Go," sung to the tune of "The Farmer in the Dell." That really made Mitchell mad. True to form, he spit at us out the open window, which only made us laugh all the more. We all waved good-bye as the police car disappeared down the road.

Also of interest, though not a colony resident as such, was a man known as Ruby the Knish Man, who visited the colony a few times a week, selling Mom's Knishes out of the back of his station wagon yelling, "Hey, knishes! Get your hot knishes! Buy a bagful and help send my wife to Florida! Hey, knishes!" People would come running, getting a taste of faraway Brooklyn right there in Loch Sheldrake. But Ruby had a falling out with the Pesekows, who apparently wanted a fee to allow him to continue selling on their property. Ruby would have no part of that. So the next time he came around, he parked his car on the shoulder of Route 52, on public property, and shouted all the more loudly, "Hey knishes! Get your hot knishes! Potato or kasha—you want 'em, I got 'em! Hey knishes!" A little increase in volume easily overcame the increase in distance. It was business as usual for Ruby for the remainder of the season.

Then there was my father, a man whose vocabulary did not contain the word "shy." He was the type of man who might have been described as quirky, one of the very few people, young or old, who wore his hair long as far back as 1958. On July 4th of that year, the Pesekows, in keeping with an annual tradition, threw a costume party, adults only, in the casino. From what I heard, things got a bit raucous. My father, perhaps bolstered by a few drinks, decided to help celebrate our nation's birthday by dressing up like an Indian. After all, he already had the hair. Since kids were banned from the festivities, I had no idea what went on inside; but the howling laughter, often accompanied by screams and yells, could be heard all over the colony, and probably half way across the lake. Apparently not satisfied with the goings-on in the casino, my father, now Chief Bernie (the only Indian ever known to have a mustache), war paint on his face, a feather in his hair, bare chested with a blanket over his shoulder, stood up in the back of Arnie Schultz's convertible, and was driven around the colony and then right through busy Loch Sheldrake, arms folded across his chest, occasionally raising his right hand and saying "How!" to the fascinated onlookers. Marty and I witnessed this first-hand, having gone into town to see if we could buy some more sparklers at Fried's or Sekofsky's. "Isn't that your father?" Marty asked, incredulous. "Yeah, that's my dad," I said, with an unlikely combination of embarrassment and pride. I don't know if he recognized me or not, but as Arnie drove slowly by, Chief Bernie waved and called out "How!" to me, and I waved back, not quite believing what I was witnessing. The man I knew worked in a factory in Harlem, sweating through the summer and freezing throughout the winter, and this was a side of him that I never knew existed. I was astonished, to say the least. The car vanished into the darkness, and I just stood there, momentarily forgetting about the sparklers, and stared at Marty, as if he would have some sort of explanation. Of course, there was none, so we both just kind of laughed, shrugged our shoulders, and eventually went about our business.

Arnie Schultz and his wife Sally were our neighbors up on the hill, and they happened to have three Mexican chihuahuas, Ricky, Impy, and ChiChi, as different from each other as day is from night. Whenever Mrs. Schultz was walking around the colony, the three little dogs were always right behind her, though she often carried ChiChi, who was bloated by excess weight and had trouble walking farther than ten feet. Impy was generally aloof and noncommittal; he didn't care what was going on. Ricky, however, would just as soon rip your face off as look at you. Innocent people who bent down to pet Ricky usually did this only once, then learned their lesson. We often brought Ricky into a conversation about South American piranhas, like what would happen if Ricky was tossed into a river infested with hungry piranhas? Who would win? It was generally conceded that it would be a close call, but that Ricky would eventually emerge picking his teeth clean with a fish bone.

Finally, there was Bart Sheridan, man among men. He was a burly young man in his twenties, who had his name hand tooled into the back of the wide leather belt he always wore.

"Bart" wasn't his real name. None of us had any idea what his real name was, but the very fact that he was actually known by a name he himself had adopted was something we found to be very impressive. The girls thought it was romantic. When Bart arrived at the colony to visit his parents and sister, everyone knew it, for no one was out of earshot of the roar of his blue and white Harley Davidson motorcycle, its chrome gleaming in the summer sun. Dark sunglasses, black military style cap, black leather jacket and black boots completed the picture. Revving the engine just for effect, we all knew Bart had arrived. Unlike fathers, who would be colony residents only on weekends and vacations, Bart seemed to live on his own schedule; he came and went according to the whims of his nature, which only added to his mystique. Occasionally, we'd actually get permission to sit on his motorcycle, which for us was a thrill beyond words.

Still, there was more to the man known as Bart. He actually owned his own horse, Chief, which he boarded at the nearby riding stables of the Hotel Evans. Every so often, Bart, his motorcycle boots traded for cowboy boots, would ride his horse through Loch Sheldrake to the colony, where those of us still recovering from the wonder of his motorcycle would be awestruck by his horse, a lustrous chestnut with a beautiful saddle and leather harness with brass appointments. Here was the whole embodiment of romantic adventure amidst our humble Catskill Mountain bungalows. Unfortunately, Bart's visits were as brief as they were unpredictable. Before long, just as mysteriously as he had arrived, Bart Sheridan would be gone, though certainly not from our impressionable imaginations, where we would see him riding off into the sunset, a true legend in his own time.

7

Revelations

After July 4th, life at the colony slowly evolved into a carefree, blissful experience for me and my friends. There was always something to do, some place to explore, some new activity to enjoy. Time itself took on an entirely different personality. The days began to lose their identities; we rarely knew the date; none of us wore a watch—timekeeping had simply become irrelevant. Every now and then there would be a new discovery, the news flashing around the colony from one kid's voice to another: a den of snakes had been found in an old stone wall; a snapping turtle had crawled onto the bank behind the handball court; there was a huge spider in a web under Bungalow 12; there was a nest behind Bungalow 15, facing the lake, that had duck eggs in it. Soon, we'd be seeing troops of tiny black and yellow ducklings following their parents across the water.

On some nights, it would be hide-and-seek in the upper meadow by the road. You wouldn't think there'd be places to hide in a meadow, but you'd be surprised. There was always someone left undiscovered out in the field, hiding in the shadows, who we knew was stealthily sneaking back towards home base to yell "Free all!" and set free those already found by the person who was "it."

On rainy nights that were not too stormy, it was hunting for night crawlers in the grass. They were huge worms that were remarkably difficult to catch, but certainly worth the effort. They'd slither partially out of their flooded holes to be grabbed with the aid of a flashlight and quick hands, then used as bait on the next fishing excursion. We all knew there were few fish who didn't see a wriggling night crawler as an irresistible meal, and a half hour or so following the flashlight's beam in the rain was a small price to pay for the prospect of some excellent fishing.

And of course, there was always the casino. The pink and gray room was lined with built-in benches around the walls, where we'd relax when we weren't dancing. Sometimes, we'd just occupy a portion of the floor in a corner of the room to talk about whatever came to mind. The jukebox was always playing, the bells and lights of the pinball machines always ringing and flashing, and there was always the counter of Pesekow's little store for candy and ice cream sandwiches.

Then, on a given day, an announcement was made that next Saturday the annual midsummer bonfire would be held at dusk. This meant that July was nearing completion. There was a pit in the far corner of the lower field by the lake where the event took place each year. All kinds of old lumber and dead tree branches were stacked in the pit, surrounded at a safe distance by most of the colony's residents. People brought lawn chairs and blankets to watch the spectacle. The fire was lit shortly after sunset, producing flames that roared skyward and sparks that danced above our heads. The intensity of the heat produced was always surprising, and people were soon seen moving their chairs and blankets further back to safer territory until things calmed down a bit later. There were lots of marshmallows to be roasted, and someone always seemed to have leftover sparklers from July 4th for the occasion. Fire-writing in the darkness was always a big hit, as was throwing the sparklers high over the lake and watching as they fell to meet their reflections in the water. There was lots of laughter, and sometimes even some singing amid the popping and crackling of the flames. Sarah had brought a blanket, and we watched the fire together from a spot just beyond the reach of the firelight. Occasionally, I got up to roast a marshmallow or two; I had a long stick to which my father had attached an old fork with some wire—it worked perfectly. Sometimes we were joined by Marty, Melanie, or Ray, but most often we were alone, which provided us with some memorable romantic moments in the semidarkness.

The bonfire festivities continued for an hour or two, and then the crowd tended to thin out, especially as parents with young children left to put their kids to bed. Soon, we also headed home as the fire was allowed to reduce to glowing embers. Without any of us really noticing, just about half the summer had slowly slipped by.

A few days after the bonfire, I was having lunch at our picnic table just outside the front door. I had opened the umbrella so that I could eat in the shade. It was a bright, sunny day, just right for eating out in the fresh air. It was my usual lunchtime fare—grape jelly on rye with a glass of milk. On the table next to my sandwich was one of my favorite *Classics Illustrated, Treasure Island*. I had read that comic probably ten times already, but I found that the real fun was in the rereading. I heard some voices coming down the path from town and looked up to see Sarah and her older sister Marilyn, carrying a couple of bags of what were probably groceries.

"Hey Sarah," I yelled, "could you come here a minute?"

She said something to her sister, handed her the bag she had been carrying, then trotted up the hill to join me at the picnic table. She was wearing a white sleeveless blouse, plaid Bermuda shorts, and sneakers, and had her hair arranged in a pony tail today, just for variety. I liked the way she looked.

"What do you want?"

"I've been having everybody write something in my autograph book, you know, from sixth grade, and I was wondering if you'd sign it too."

"Sure I would. Go ahead and get it. While you're inside I'll finish your sandwich for you."

"Better not," I said, looking back from the screen door. I went inside, got the book from my dresser, searched for a pen but couldn't find one, so I grabbed a pencil that was on the kitchen table and went back outside to the picnic table, where Sarah was happily chewing a mouthful of grape jelly on rye.

"Hey! What're you doing?"

"Eating. I'm hungry. This is pretty good."

I tried to feign anger, but it just wasn't there. In fact, I kind of liked the fact that she was enjoying my sandwich. I opened to the last unsigned page in the book, and handed her the pencil. After taking a few gulps of my milk, she glanced at the book's other pages, to see what kind of things had already been written, then started work on her own. I watched with great interest while she wrote.

"Hey, don't look," she cried, covering the book with her arm so I couldn't see.

"Why not?"

"You just can't, that's all. Don't look until later, okay? Promise?"

I agreed, though it made me all the more curious to see what she wrote. She finished in a moment, closed the book, and handed me the pencil. "Remember, don't you dare look," she said, as she got up and ran down the driveway and out of sight. I didn't want to embarrass her, so I didn't look—at least not right away. When I was sure she was gone, I opened the book to her page and read what she had written:

> Remember Grant, remember Lee,
> But most of all, remember me.

She signed her name and had added an additional message: Read *"Isle of View,"* a book I didn't recognize, but would look for back in the Bronx.

That afternoon, we all went swimming, along with lots of other kids and a few teenagers, who more or less left us alone.

I was just fooling around in my inner tube in pretty deep water, kind of lost in thought—a routine situation for me; my father called it being in a trance—with my legs dangling beneath me. Sarah kept swimming underwater and tickling my feet. I tried kicking at her, but she was just too fast, surfacing a distance away and saying that it wasn't her, it was fish. So the next time she tried it, I slid out from my inner tube and took off after her underwater. I managed to grab her foot and started tickling like crazy. I could see her writhing in all directions, trying to break free, air bubbles bursting from her nose and mouth. We both surfaced, Sarah screaming and laughing at the same time. "That was so mean," she yelled, and started splashing me, so I splashed back. Marty swam over between us, the white tee shirt his mother made him wear to guard against sunburn plastered to his body. He looked at me disapprovingly, and said, "What are you two doing?"

"Nothing, Marty, nothing at all," said Sarah, who sent one more splash in my direction, and then swam off. Marty turned back to me, still scowling, and asked, "What's with you two any-how?" This was something he'd asked before. I just shrugged my shoulders and swam off in Sarah's direction.

The next day, I dropped by Marty's bungalow and was met at the door by his mother, who told me that Marty was being punished by not being allowed outdoors right now, and that he'd see me some time later. I wasn't exactly a stranger to punishment myself, but it was usually for refusing to eat my supper, or some other food-related crime. I wondered what he'd done. Before going back home, I stopped by his bedroom window, where he told me the details through the screen in the softest of whispers. He had been yelling obscenities at his poor maiden aunt, who lived with them. This was not terribly unusual; Marty did that a lot. I happened to be on hand for a number of his anti-aunt tirades. But this time, his mother happened to be right outside hanging laundry on the line and she heard the whole thing. Denial was futile. I would not be seeing Marty for a while.

So I decided that this was a good opportunity to sneak off to live my other, totally secret and private life, unknown to everyone except my mother. Back at our bungalow, I told her about Marty, and then said that I was heading out.

"Where're you going?"

"I thought I'd go to Texas."

That was all she needed to know. If asked where I was, her answer would be "Out," and no amount of cross-examination would get her to reveal any further information. She was good when it came to keeping secrets.

"Oh, I see. Well, just be careful over there, and don't be too long."

"Don't worry. I'll be fine. I'll be back before lunch," I said, and walked out the door.

I headed into Loch Sheldrake, always making sure that I wasn't being followed. I crossed the road in front of The Strand, walked up the street to Kove's, then went through their parking lot and walked into the woods out back. In a little while, I came to a narrow dirt road going down hill away from the Hotel Evans in the general direction of their lake. Then the woods opened up into a large clearing, and I was at my destination. It was the Evans riding stables. I had come upon this little patch of the West some weeks earlier when on a solitary scouting expedition to a previously unexplored area. There were two barns, a large corral, a walking ring, lots of horses, and three or four men who wore cowboy boots and cowboy hats and didn't fit the general description of people renting bungalows for the summer. They all had ruddy complexions that seemed to indicate a lot of time outdoors; two or three were in their twenties, and one, the guy in charge, looked about twice that, but sometimes it's hard to tell. I imagined right away that this is what it must be like to live in Texas.

We all knew such a place existed somewhere, for Bart Sheridan kept his horse, Chief, boarded there. But we never bothered to look. The interest just wasn't there. The treasure, however, once uncovered, was too good to be shared. I wanted to keep this amazing discovery to myself.

I started out haunting the fringes of the ranch, as I liked to call it, then gradually moved in closer over several visits to where they let me pet the horses, then hold their bridles while they were being saddled up, and then, the ultimate pleasure of all, to be allowed to slowly walk the horses around the walking ring to cool them off after a ride. The men seemed to get a charge out of the fact that I liked to do what they called work; rarely, however, were they interested in engaging in any conversation, other than learning my name, and occasionally saying something like "Hey Philip—put this inside the barn, okay?"

The horses were the absolute gentlest of creatures, and seemed to be in a perpetual state of slumber, even when awake. And I loved them. I loved the way they looked, the way they felt, the way they smelled. How could I share this? I was living a secret life as a pretend wrangler. How I wished I had cowboy boots instead of sneakers, and a hat to match. Then I'd blend right in, and all the hotel guests coming down there for horseback rides would think I was just one of the men.

All the horses were named for spices and such usually found in the kitchen—Sugar, Cinnamon, Pepper, Rosemary—that sort of thing. The main barn had a central corridor with stalls on either side, and was always dark and cool, even on hot days. Up above was a loft with lots of hay bales stacked to the rafters. Nearby was a smaller barn and corral that housed boarded horses for the summer, like Chief, who I visited often. I knew it was selfish to keep the ranch from my friends, but also realized that these men probably wouldn't be too happy with a bunch of kids hanging out at their workplace. So my double life as bungalow kid and Texas cowboy remained a secret, and persisted right through to the end of summer.

There was something else that I kept a secret, once again from everyone except my mother, with whom I shared just about everything. It involved a visit to Sekofsky's. My friend Ray had told me that Sekofsky's was selling comic books this year as well as Fried's. I hadn't noticed this on my previous trips to the store, probably because I was so afraid of running into my nemesis there, the old man, that I kept my eyes glued to the floor. Ray said they had a couple of revolving racks near the back of the store, and there were some *Classics Illustrated* there that he felt I should check out. He knew they were my favorite. So despite my fear of a skirmish with the enemy, I decided to give it a shot.

The first thing I did upon entering the store was to look over toward the fishing counter to see if he was there. To my surprise, not only was he not there, but no one else was either. They must be short handed. I was in luck. An immediate wave of relief washed over me, and I felt that I could peruse their comics in a state of ease and comfort. I found their display right where Ray had described it to me; it was the usual collection of Batman and Superman, cartoon characters for little kids, and quite a few *Classics Illustrated*. Thumbing through this latter group, I was astonished to find one that I had been looking for for over a year—*Moby Dick*. I had seen the movie two summers before, right next door at the Strand. I was only around ten then, and didn't understand everything that well, but liked the movie a lot anyway. I'd been looking for this comic ever since. I knew it existed. Fortunately, I had the fifteen cents on me, and I looked through the colorful pages as I walked towards the cash register. Some dialogue involving Captain Ahab caught my attention, and for a moment it seemed like the captain himself was actually addressing me: "Well, if it isn't my best customer." Looking up, I couldn't have been more shocked if I had been harpooned. It was the old man. He had moved over to another section of the store, working the main cash register. He never seemed to change his outfit—his white shirt and suspenders were a staple of his wardrobe. He was looking at me from behind his rimless glasses, grinning as if he knew the world's choicest secret. I became so scared that I briefly thought about dropping the comic and running outside. But before I could act, he said, "What've you got there?"

"Um, *Mo-Moby Dick*," I stuttered.

"Oh yeah? What's it about? And speak up!"

"Um, this guy, and he's hunting this whale."

"Really. Why's he doing that?"

"It bit his leg off once."

"No kidding. How'd it happen?"

"I think he was trying to kill it."

"Ahh. Revenge then."

"Yeah, I guess."

"Tell me something. Do you remember a guy named Starbuck, his first mate?"

I shook my head yes, though actually, I couldn't remember anyone's name from the movie except Ahab, but I was surprised the old man knew any of them.

"In one scene, he says to Captain Ahab, 'Vengeance on a dumb brute, that simply smote thee from blindest instinct, seems blasphemous.' Or something like that. Blasphemous means something that's insulting to God. Remember that. I want you to think about it. I'm sure it's in your comic book there, in one form or another. When you come across that scene, stop reading and think about what it might mean, okay?"

I didn't say anything, because I was struck speechless by this outpouring of information from a man who had been so hostile to me on our earlier encounters. I didn't know what was going on, or what to say. My sweaty hand was starting to wrinkle the cover of the comic book, so I set it down on the counter. I just stood there, staring at him, and my confusion must have been pretty apparent on my face. How could he know anything about a movie I saw two years ago?

"What're you so shocked about? You know, I was a professor once, a teacher in a college. I knew literature as well as you know fishing tackle."

I was in shock. Somehow, I never pictured the old man as anything but an old man.

"You take that comic book home, and read it. Then, if you want to talk about it, come in the store here and look me up. Any time. If you don't see me, you can ask for me. My name is Samuel. You hear?"

Did I ever. I told him my name was Philip. I thought for a moment about shaking his hand; I was never sure when to do that and when not to. However, in a moment, he reached his hand across the counter to shake mine, and I felt like the world tilted a bit to one side. This was so different from the man at the fishing department; maybe that guy was his evil twin. But this man in front of me was smiling, actually smiling, as I gave him my fifteen cents for the comic. He never said "heh?" or gave me any annoyed looks, or said anything resembling nasty. Maybe I just didn't know who the man was on our earlier meetings, and maybe he didn't really know me either. But all that seemed to change right there and then. Maybe it changed a bit when I was in the store buying those Eagle Claw hooks a while back with Marty. I wasn't sure. Emboldened by his good mood, I decided to take a chance. I asked him how come he was being so nice to me. What he did kind of surprised me. He looked at me, but didn't say anything. I thought at first that maybe he didn't hear me. So I pressed on. "Was it because of what happened when my friend and me came in here to buy those hooks that time?"

"What do you think?"

"I don't know. But—you knew they cost forty-nine cents, didn't you," more a statement than a question.

"I guess we both knew that, didn't we?" he said, and I shook my head in agreement. One thing I was very sure about was that I would go into that store many more times over the course of the summer, and we would talk about not only *Moby Dick*, but also other books I had read and enjoyed, and even Frederic Chopin, who he knew quite a lot about. One thing for certain—I would never have to be afraid of the old man again. He was my friend now, and a valuable resource as well. I walked back home that day with my *Classics Illustrated* tucked under my arm, my emotions still a bit confused, but my state of mind much more content and at peace than before, and more than a little bit changed.

8

Encounters

The next morning, I awoke to rain falling outside my window. I had moved my pillow to the foot of the bed, where the window was, so that I could see directly outside, and feel the evening air on my face as I fell off to sleep. This morning, that air was cold and damp, but I hesitated to lower the window, listening instead to the sound of rain on the grass, a gentle, soothing sound unheard in the Bronx. The window screen was wet, and I reached up to the wet spots, sliding the water into various temporary patterns with my forefinger before pulling the window down to shut out the cold air. I heard my mother get out of bed on the other side of the room and put on her heavy bathrobe for warmth. The bungalow had no heat, and though I couldn't see, I knew she would soon head for the kitchen and turn on the gas oven to make the place more comfortable.

Breakfast this morning was a hushed affair since my sister Sheila was still sleeping. She had gone with some friends the night before over to Brown's Hotel, a few miles up the road, because there was a rumor floating around that Jerry Lewis himself was staying there—he always said that Brown's was his "favorite resort"—but I didn't know how things turned out. My mother said that Sheila got back pretty late, so our conversation was limited to whispers. Once I was finished with breakfast, however, I quietly prepared to go outside, despite the weather. Though it was well into summer, this kind of day in the mountains called for a flannel shirt, jacket, and even a baseball cap to ward off the elements. The rain had subsided to a misty drizzle, and my mother wanted me to carry an umbrella to keep dry. I made it quite clear, however, that I would rather die than be seen walking around carrying an umbrella. That sort of thing could ruin a kid for life. She relented, and I went out the door.

On the way down the hill, I saw Mr. Sheridan, Bart's father, fishing from the pier, his huge steel tackle box at his feet. He was one of the nicest grownups I knew, and I was never reluctant or afraid to talk to him, or ask him a question. This morning, he was all decked out in yellow rain gear, and seemed totally unfazed by the persistent drizzle, which I could hear making a hissing sound on the lake's calm surface. The shore on the far side was completely invisible, covered by heavy fog.

"Hi, Mr. Sheridan."

"Hello, Philip. How we doing today?" Not waiting for an answer, he continued, "You know, sometimes the best fishing's in the rain. The bass'll come right to the surface to feed, 'cause it gets dark down there without any sunshine. That's why I'm using a floater. Looks like a little frog swimming. No bites yet, but I'm hopeful."

I stood on the pier next to him and watched him cast out a few times. I'd often thought of asking him what it was like having a son who was a legend, but never did. I thought I might get some pointers on how to go about becoming a legend myself, but somehow never had the courage to ask. I was about to turn around and say goodbye when for some reason I stopped myself before I took another step.

"Mr. Sheridan? How's your son?"

"Bart? Oh, he's okay, I'm sure. He's not here now, you know," reeling in his line.

"I know, but I was wondering. He's a really cool guy and all. Me and my friends really like him. And well, how come . . . I mean, why does he, um, where is he now?"

Mr. Sheridan didn't respond. Instead, he raised his rod, took a long look at his lure, and cast out again.

"Why do you want to know?"

"I don't know, it's just that we all think he's a neat guy, like I said, and well, I'd like to be like him some day."

"You would?" he said, nodding as if his thoughts were far away. "Well, nothing's easy, you know." Silence then, Mr. Sheridan reeling in his lure to make it look like a frog swimming. "A cool guy to you, a puzzle to me."

"Oh." It was all I could think of to say, as I had no idea what he meant. I was kind of sorry I'd asked in the first place, so I started to go, but once again changed my mind. "Doesn't he like it here?"

"Oh, I suppose he likes it, though not as much as, say, you do."

"I like it all right."

"What do you like, specifically?"

"Well, fishing, and swimming, doing stuff with my friends, and just being in the country and all. You know what my father says about me? 'The kid sees grass, he goes crazy.' "

"That's pretty funny," he said, chuckling at the thought.

"I think it's because of where we live—in the Bronx. The nearest patch of grass is in Claremont Park, about ten blocks away. That's where the trees are, too."

"Well then, you might be right about that. Hey, you know, I was just thinking. Why don't you go get your rod and come down here and join me? I'll let you use one of my lures. I bet the fish'll be getting pretty hungry soon."

"Maybe I will in a little while, okay? I want to go see if my friend Marty's in the casino."

"Oh, I see. Well, maybe another time. See you later, then."

I wished him luck fishing and turned to go on to the casino. Right away, I felt pretty bad. I thought he was disappointed that

I didn't want to fish with him. I looked back over my shoulder as I walked away, and kind of saw a lonely man fishing in the rain, without his son, the legend. I thought for a moment to run back home and get my rod, but the thought was fleeting, and I continued toward the casino, where I could plainly hear someone playing pinball.

Marty was inside, lying on his back on the bench next to the jukebox; some teenagers were gathered around the pinball machine. I sat down next to him and asked, "What's going on?"

"Nothing much. I got a few nickels from my mother to play some pinball, but what's-his-face over there's been hogging it all morning."

What's-his-face. Mitchell Black, who was pounding the edges of the horse racing machine hard enough to cause it to "tilt," which would shut if off. He didn't seem too happy, probably having lost a bunch of nickels playing that particular game, which, as I've mentioned before, was pretty addictive. I knew there'd be trouble when he looked over his shoulder at us and yelled out, "Hey stretch! Lend me a quarter and maybe I won't kick your ass for what you said to me when I borrowed your basketball that time."

My first impulse was to break for the door, but I knew I wouldn't make it before he did. I looked at Marty, who was pretty good at coming up with plans of action in emergencies like this one, but he didn't seem to have an idea this time. I started to get really scared, picturing myself with a bloody face lying unconscious on the floor, my pockets turned inside out. Mitchell started coming across the room toward us, looking threatening enough for an entire gang of bullies. "Well, how 'bout it, you little punk? What's it gonna be?"

Terrified, I said, "Look, Mitchell. I'm broke. But my mother is in the card room playing mah jong with her friends, and I'll get you the money from her. Okay?" And I started walking toward the card room door, with Marty adding, "I'll walk ya."

"You better be back in ten seconds or I'm coming after ya," he said, as we went into the card room and shut the door behind us. Of course, there was no one in the card room, but there was a separate entrance, which was right where we headed, softly opening and then closing the door, and running like mad across the grass to disappear behind the handball court, completely out of breath, more from fear than running. It was then that the laughter began, probably just releasing the tension from that encounter in the casino.

"How could anyone that big be so stupid," I said, struggling to get the words out while laughing uncontrollably. Marty stuck his upper teeth out over his lower lip and said in his best Bugs Bunny voice, "What a maroon!" This got us laughing all the more, but we managed to stifle our hysterics in case the thugs decided to come looking for us, which we felt was a real possibility. So we thought it best to quickly head back up the hill among the bungalows, where at least there would be witnesses to any carnage. I certainly wanted to put some time and distance between me and Mitchell, since I seemed to be the object of most of his wrath, so we both made up to just head home for now, and then get together again later.

I carefully returned to my bungalow, looking all around me with each step I took. No one seemed to be following. I was relieved to get in the door, where the warmth from the oven felt really good and comforting. My mother and sister were playing cards at the kitchen table, and I joined them for a few hands of gin rummy, then went inside the bedroom and stretched out on. my bed to read some more of *Moby Dick* while the gray mists continued to swirl past the window panes.

About ten minutes or so later, far out to sea, the Pequod was lowering her boats to chase a small pod of whales off to larboard. I wasn't sure what that meant exactly, but I loved every moment of it. Queequeg was in the bow of the lead boat readying his harpoon when my mother asked, "Where's your hat?" She was standing in the bedroom doorway holding my jacket, which I had unceremoniously tossed in a heap on a chair. It's funny how a room that was warm and comfortable (not to mention far out in the Pacific) could change to become cold and clammy in an instant. Tiny beads of sweat began to form along my hairline, as I realized where my hat was. And it wasn't in the bungalow. When I sat down next to Marty in the casino, I had taken off my hat and placed it next to me on the bench. That's where it was, in the casino, with Mitchell Black and his pals.

"Um, my hat? Uh, I think I must've left it somewhere."

"Where? Where'd you go?"

"The casino, I think."

"You think? What's the matter? You can't remember where you went?"

"Oh, no. I remember alright. I'm pretty sure it was the casino."

"Well why don't you go get it, before it disappears."

"Okay. I will. Maybe after lunch."

"No, not after lunch. Now. It'll take you two minutes."

"Okay. I *will*." But I didn't move. I turned back to the comic book, pretending to be so absorbed in the story that I couldn't possibly be torn away from the action for even two minutes. But it didn't work. Every colorful square now meant nothing to me, and one way or another, my mother knew it. With another tone of voice entirely, one that I knew meant business, she told me to put on my jacket, go down the hill to the casino, get my hat, and come back for lunch. Delay was not an option. As I slipped on my sneakers and took my jacket from my mother, I walked out the door feeling like a condemned criminal walking down that shadowy corridor to The Chair. There was no turning back. I thought, as I walked, that this might be a good time to run away from home. I could live in the woods and eat nuts and berries and stuff. Sure, I thought. Good idea. With each step down the hill, I came closer and closer to my doom. There was no plan, no strategy, no escape. In complete and utter desperation, I resorted to prayer. What I really needed now was a miracle. I needed to have Mitchell and his friends gone, and my hat on the bench where I left it. If only that would happen, it would be truly miraculous.

I walked up the two steps onto the casino patio and looked in through the first window, hoping that the divine intervention I longed for had occurred. But my hopes came crashing to the floor when I saw that Mitchell was still there, with his friends, in a booth next to the pinball machines, and not only that, he was wearing my hat.

I pulled the screen door open and took a few faltering steps in their direction. Mitchell was only too pleased to see me.

"Well look who's here. You got my quarter?" When I didn't respond, he continued. "What's the matter? Lose something?"

"Yeah, my hat."

"This hat? You're wrong, punk. This happens to be my hat. Didn't you ever hear of finders weepers?" It's finders keepers, you big jerk, I thought. My hands were starting to shake from nervousness.

"It . . . it's my hat." Despite my best efforts to stop them, tears began to well up in my eyes. I was ashamed and embarrassed, and did everything I could to prevent a tear from running down my cheek. I was now just a few feet from Mitchell, and I thought, insanely, of how a frog can shoot out its tongue lightning fast to snatch a bug off a leaf. If only I could move my arm that fast, I could grab my hat and run out the door. He'd never catch me. As if he were reading my mind, he said, "Try for this hat, and I'll break your arm." And he leaned a bit forward, actually closing the gap between me and the hat, tempting me to try it. He knew just what he was doing. I felt my whole body shaking now. My ears were ringing, and I discovered, much to my dismay, that I really had to pee. My despair by now had turned to panic, and I thought momentarily of just turning and running out the door. I'd have to live in shame and humiliation for the rest of my life, but I'd get used to it. Strangely, with the moment of crisis upon me, I inexplicably did just the opposite. I darted my hand out for the hat, and felt Mitchell's iron grip on my wrist.

"What are you, stupid? I told you what I'd do if you made a grab for the hat." He started to twist my arm, just as if he would break it. His strength and the force of his clamp on my wrist was incredible. He wrenched my arm behind my back, continuing to twist and push my arm upward. I had no thoughts but for the pain, which had become excruciating. I thought my bones would soon start to fracture, and my joints come apart. The tears started to come back. The only thing left for me was to scream, which I was about to do, when something totally unexpected occurred.

At first, I thought the voice was descending from the heavens by the powers above. The words were indistinct. I could barely hear them in my distress, but their meaning was clear and true.

"Leave him alone."

The source of the statement was not above, as I briefly suspected, but below, coming from Mitchell's own table. Sitting across from him, taking a few last drags on his cigarette before stubbing it out in the ashtray, was Mel Minkoff, master Krepsi storyteller. Blowing a long stream of smoke up into the air above Mitchell's head, he very nonchalantly added, "Let him go or I'll break *your* arm."

Mitchell released me without saying a word. The agony in my arm subsided, but left it hurting just the same. I was struck absolutely dumb by the sudden intervention, though not that dumb. I managed to swipe my hat off his head. I was in shock, staring at Mel, then Mitchell, then back to Mel. The mysteries of the power structure working within the average teenage gang of thugs grew deeper and more complex. The boisterous, loud-mouthed bully was just a figurehead. "You're still a little punk," Mitchell said, his face a picture of depraved disappointment. I knew it was risky, but I just couldn't stop myself from saying in a reasonably calm, though still pretty unsteady voice, "And you know what you are? Insulting to God!"

Mel stifled a laugh, and I looked at him with a considerable degree of awe and astonishment. With the slightest movement of his head, he suggested I get lost. Which I did, without hesitation, trying to understand, perhaps without success, yet another aspect of the intricacies of human relationships. I was out the door and into the fog and drizzle in a second, my hat placed firmly atop my head, hurrying back up the hill to the safety and warmth of Bungalow 19.

9

Blueberry Hill

July had turned into August, and before long it was time for blueberry-picking up on the hill across the road. On a given day in mid-August, we decided to raid our kitchens of the largest pots available, and head across the road and up the hill. We were all going, including Ray and another girl who was a late-comer to the colony, Barbara. The particular path we took was of little consequence. The idea was to get up there, where the entire hilltop was covered with high-bush blueberries, fat and juicy, just ripening in the sun and waiting for us to begin the harvest. The longer, though easier route, would take us through town and then behind some stores and houses on the far side of the street. That way was a gentler route to the top. Today, however, we were anxious to get going, so we went directly across the road and up the hill behind the bungalows of a smaller colony known as the Sunshine Cottages. This route was shorter, but steeper, and was often hard work climbing. It was a pretty warm and kind of humid day; my mother warned me that thunder-storms were in the forecast. No one seemed to mind the heat, though, and we worked our way up the heavily wooded slope, occasionally climbing on or around rocks and good-sized boulders that blocked our way. Eventually, however, we made it to the top, which was much more open, and were able to take in the view. From there, the lake was an azure jewel almost entirely surrounded by green forest. Only right below us was there human activity—the town, the colony, the Lakeside Hotel. Across the lake we could just make out Chinese Alley, and occasional speed boats and water skiers leaving white curving wakes across the water. Sometimes the sound of a car horn would reach us, but little else. We all went right to work picking blueberries, the sound of the berries plunking into the empty pots making us laugh. Conversation was at a minimum, except when someone would happen upon a particularly full bush, which we'd all gather around and pick clean.

In a little while, we all sat down in a grassy clearing up there, eating blueberries and picking out the hard, green unripe berries which somehow always got in, and tossing them aside. Occasionally, one would be tossed in my direction and bounce off the side of my face. This would mark the start of a small berry war, with berries flying in all directions, regardless of who started the hostilities. The girls, however, with cooler temperaments, would usually stop the warfare, especially when the ammunition turned to ripe berries, and the threat of stains was imminent.

Later on, with our pots filled to capacity, Sarah and I were sitting next to each other, taking advantage of the shade provided by a particularly large bush, just relaxing and enjoying the peacefulness of the hilltop. I don't remember what we were talking about, just talking. At one point, looking at her, I realized that for whatever reason, her mood had changed. I didn't understand it. She was leaning on one elbow, picking at some grass and tossing it aside. Without turning to me, she said, "You know, I love it up here. I really love it. I wish I could stay here forever." And after a momentary pause, "With you." I was nodding in agreement with her, but stopped when I heard those final two words. I wasn't sure what she meant. No girl had ever said anything like that to me, and it left me kind of bewildered.

How does one respond? What did she mean by "up here?" On this hilltop? At Pesekow's? And most of all, what was she saying by adding "with you?" Her eyes were averted, but moving slightly, I could see that they were moist. She was on the verge of tears, and it made me kind of nervous. I should have asked her to explain; I should have understood what she meant in the first place, but didn't. I could have asked her all of that, and could have said so many things, but true to form, I resisted, saying instead "I know, Sarah. I know just what you mean," when in fact, I just didn't get it. I reached for her hand, wondering if that was the right thing, the appropriate thing, to say. Before more could be said, though, Melanie came over with Marty to bring our attention to the fact that the weather had been changing, and maybe we should think about starting back. Sure enough, looking up from Sarah, I saw that the lake was no longer blue, but dark gray, and the sky had clouded over considerably. We both got up, carefully picked up our filled-to-the-brim pots of berries, and we all started back down the hill as a distant rumble of thunder was heard in the heavens somewhere behind us. At that, we all tried to pick up our pace. I knew that thunder meant the presence of lightning, and that a hilltop was the wrong place to be. So we worked our way down the slope through the trees as best as we could. Going back down was actually harder than the trip up, for we were all conscious of not spilling our precious cargo. My mind, however, was not so much on the berries, as it was on Sarah, directly in front of me.

As we got further down the hill, it became amazingly dark in the woods as the wind began to pick up. We found ourselves tripping and stumbling over roots and rocks, losing blueberries, and before long, losing our way. We were walking far too long. Where were the Sunshine Cottages? We stopped walking. The sound of the wind in the trees had quickly become a loud roar accompanied by heavy rain hitting the canopy of leaves above us. Not that much rain was making it through to where we were standing, but we knew that situation wouldn't last much longer. We were all pretty scared by this point, and "What should we do?" was the question before us. The trees were swaying in all different directions, and we stood there, not knowing what to do.

A decision was made to go a little further down, inching our way along the slope. Finally, a bungalow came into view through the trees, but it was white, not yellow. The Sunshine Cottages were yellow. As we stood there, now starting to get pretty wet, we became aware of a large, black mass looming up before us out of the gloom. Marty yelled, "What the hell is that?" which didn't help matters all that much. Now we were really frightened, and almost started to go back up the hill to escape this latest threat when we heard the sound of a car horn, and it didn't seem to be that far off. We chose to continue just a bit further down the hill in the direction of the horn, and it didn't take too long to solve the mystery of where we were.

We were on the hill that rose up behind Rosenblatt's Esso station, a large building built into the hillside, its huge back wall just becoming visible through the forest. The bungalow was one of a handful the Rosenblatts rented during the summer. Somehow, in our haste to get down the hill, we had become disoriented in the semidarkness and drifted a bit to the south. Rather than continue downhill, we decided to keep to the relative shelter of the woods, head back north, parallel to the unseen road, until we came to the Sunshine Cottages, which finally appeared before us in a little while, much to our relief. There was no choice now but to head directly into the open and dash across the road to safety. The wind and rain was unrelenting as we crossed the road and finally entered Pesekow's. We were all soaked to the skin.

With our pots still pretty full of berries, we really couldn't run, so we all walked as quickly as possible, in six different directions heading for shelter, some of us yelling out "See you later" as we went. Crashes of thunder and flashes of lightning were all around us. Somehow though, I felt that I couldn't go into my bungalow just yet, even though I was right outside in the driveway, and well aware that my mother must be really worried about where I was. Putting my pot of berries down on the grass, I continued down the hill a ways so I could watch

Sarah heading for her place. I found myself splashing through the water that was streaming down the driveway. Finally, I just stood there, hoping that she would look back over her shoulder and see me watching her. I thought for a moment to call out her name, but felt that she'd never hear me amid the rain and wind in the pines, so I didn't. Sarah never turned, but entered her bungalow, leaving me trying to make some sense of the state of my emotions and her emotions, and what exactly was happening to us.

A loud crash of thunder broke me out of my reverie and I ran back up the hill, picked up the berries, and went inside, where, as I suspected, my mother had been worried sick about me out in the storm. I told her everything that happened, though left out anything about Sarah. She wanted to know why we didn't go into Rosenblatt's until the storm passed, but I had no answer for her. I guess we were just too scared. She was delighted, however, with the harvest of blueberries, but appalled to see that I was soaked to the skin. I was actually dripping all over the kitchen floor, so she shooed me into the bedroom with strict orders to change my clothes completely and not come out until I was dry. So I went inside and began the process of peeling off the wet clothes and warming myself up. All the while, I was listening to the rain beating a pattern on the roof, watching it dripping off the eaves, and looking out the back window in the direction of Sarah's bungalow, dimly visible in the pines.

The next morning was one of those delightfully cool and clear days where the world seems to have been washed clean by the recent rains. After my morning bowl of Cheerios, with Peppy perched on the edge of my bowl to help himself to my milk, I told my mother that I would be out fishing for a while, and she told me there'd be homemade blueberry jam waiting for me when I returned. I had thought about going to Texas that morning; certainly no one would find me there. But I changed my mind, thinking that I didn't want to be that far away from the prospect of blueberry jam for lunch. I grabbed my rod and equipment and what remained of my worm collection in a coffee can I kept under the bungalow, and headed down toward the lake. I wanted to be by myself this morning, for I had some things to think about, with Sarah topping the list. And I didn't want to see her, at least not yet.

One of the nice things about the colony was that it was on the west side of the lake, and the bungalows were on a slope facing east. On a morning like this, the lake was all aglitter with sunlight dancing amid the ripples. I knew a spot that was really private in the wooded area between the Lakeside Hotel and Chinese Alley, and I decided to head there. It was one of those secret places I'd go to when I wanted to be by myself—just a little open space of shoreline where one could sit on the bank and fish and enjoy the beauty of the lake on a morning like this.

So that's where I went to fish and think. I didn't even care if I caught anything. It didn't really matter. I had a pretty good cast out into the water and just sat in the morning sun and watched my red and white bobber adrift in the wavelets. It didn't take long for my thoughts to turn to Sarah. The thing is, I just didn't understand girls very well, I admitted to myself. Sarah in particular. She was a great girl, really pretty, as I've said before, and wonderful to be around. We had lots of fun going to the movies, dancing at the Lakeside or the casino, swimming in the lake, or just hanging out. I liked holding her when we danced. She liked it, too. I could tell. She liked me, and I liked her, but apparently, something else was happening here that I was only dimly aware of. I was sure it was no big deal; it was just that every now and then, she became so emotional. And lately, I found myself reacting to her emotions, and matching them, too. I wasn't exactly sure what that meant. I kept thinking about what she said atop the hill yesterday, and tying that in with the conversation Marty and I had had that time in that tunnel underneath Route 52, about how girls were always thinking about getting married and such.

I guessed that the right thing to do at this point, the only logical thing, would be to just go on exactly as if nothing happened at all. In truth, I didn't know what else to do, in that I really didn't understand why she said what she did. And few things are more unnerving to a guy than a girl crying in his presence. Maybe I should simply pretend that nothing happened. We had a fun time picking berries, and got caught in the rain. I'll let her make the next move, though I had no idea what that next move might be.

I continued to fish that morning, if for no other reason than it was so enjoyable and peaceful. But before long, my stomach was telling me lunchtime was approaching, and I decided to return to the colony. After walking about twenty minutes or so, I was back, going up the hill, cutting through the pines to get home, when a voice called out to me—it was Sarah; she was sitting on the front porch of Bungalow 4.

"Philip! Philip! Wait up!" She came down off her porch, and we met in the grassy area between bungalows. "How're you doing? I see you finally dried off," she said when she was closer.

"Oh, yeah, I'm all dried off, all right. I had to change all my clothes, though. How about you?"

"Same here. My mother yelled at me for not coming back sooner. She was pretty angry. Catch anything?"

"Couple of perch. Threw 'em back."

"Oh." Then, after a brief pause, "It's nice out today, isn't it?"

"Yeah, it sure is."

Then there was a brief, awkward moment of silence and head bobbing that seemed to last ten minutes, but was probably only ten seconds. We both kind of looked around, our eyes darting everywhere but at each other. There were benches placed between the bungalows, facing manicured rectangles of grass and flowering shrubs. Sarah looked in the direction of the one near her bungalow and asked if I wanted to sit with her for a few minutes. I didn't see any real harm, so we sat down, and I placed my fishing rod on the ground, where I became overly interested in my sneakers, examining their many and varied characteristics as long as possible.

"You know, I really like you, Philip." Having no precise idea in which direction this would go, I decided to stay silent, my sneakers still absorbing my undivided attention, though I was fully aware that Sarah was looking at me, and nowhere else.

"I was so excited to see you back in June on the patio that day. I wanted to look my best. I wanted us to pick up where we left off the year before."

"Oh yeah, I remember. You really looked nice that day," I said, recalling her lipstick, and blushing a little at the memory.

"I think what we have between us is very special," she said, "and I just wanted you to know that. I wanted you to know how I feel, that's all."

I looked at her sitting beside me. Her long brown hair had a sunlit glow, and her summer tanned face, her arms and hands had the appearance of a soft warm cloth, even nicer than Mr. Green's pants. Sarah had become so much prettier in the two months since that morning on the patio. She didn't need the lipstick.

"I know what you're saying, Sarah. I like you too. A lot," I said, smiling, just briefly meeting her eyes. Then, as I tried to do yesterday atop the hill, I reached for her hand, and held it. I didn't care who saw. She looked down, then at me, smiling as radiant a smile as I'd ever seen. Her smile made me feel so good. Nothing more was said, nothing more was needed to be said, for many minutes. Finally, as if she just thought of something else to say, Sarah said, "The Fireman's Ball is coming soon. I'm really looking forward to it. We're going, right?"

"Oh, yeah, of course. I can't wait."

"Well that's great! It'll be so much fun. I'm going to wear my blue dress. I've been saving it all summer." Then, after a somewhat thoughtful pause, "You gonna go swimming later?"

"I guess so. After lunch."

"Okay, great. Well, I'll see you down at the lake later, okay?"

"Sure. I'll see you later, Sarah."

And that was that. She got up and went back to her bungalow. I could tell from the way she was walking that she was feeling pretty good about our conversation, and I felt pretty good too, as I said. I went back up the driveway to my bungalow with a clear head and a light step, thinking about how Sarah had become not just a good friend, but a good girlfriend. It was a terrific feeling.

About twenty feet away from my bungalow, I could smell the promised blueberry jam my mother had been preparing through the morning. Each summer, my mother made the most delicious jam from the berries I picked. Even now, I can still recall the taste, the texture, the aroma of that dark purple jam on a piece of fresh Wonder Bread. And on that particular morning, I was able to enter the bungalow like a new man; I let the screen door slam behind me, and I sat down at the kitchen table prepared for an absolutely wonderful lunch.

10

No Sadness

There were actually two events that occurred in August that made the month extra special. One was the annual Fireman's Ball that Sarah had referred to, and the other was my birthday, this year my twelfth. I was never one for subtle hints about an appropriate gift for a person whose qualities and attainments were well documented, so I went straight for the bottom line—I wanted a Gilbert combination chemistry set and microscope kit. I even had a picture of it that I tore out of a magazine, and handed to my father the week before. After an initial sarcastic comment like, "What are you gonna do, blow the place up?" he took the picture and said he'll see what he could do.

Sure enough, on the Friday night before my birthday, my father, just up from the city for the weekend, came into the bungalow carrying a metal box by its built-in handle that I recognized immediately. Not only was it the precise set I wanted, but it came with the added bonus of live shrimp eggs that I could nurture until they hatched, then watch develop and grow, all under the microscope. It was almost too exciting to imagine. By the next morning, I created the proper liquid environment for the tiny tan shrimp eggs, poured some into the little dish provided, and sat back and waited. Part of the kit was a log, so I could record the hour-by-hour changes taking place. I even woke myself up in the middle of the night and quietly crept into the kitchen to view and record the momentous events: 2 A.M.—no change; 5 A.M.—eggs rounder, swelling; 11 A.M.—some eggs showing movement inside; 3 P.M.—baby shrimp struggling to emerge from eggs; 7 P.M.—I'm a father! Baby shrimp swimming around all over the dish!

Every now and then, friends of my parents would stop by, take a look in the microscope, and want to know when they'd be invited over for shrimp dinner. My own friends dropped by as well, showing remarkable interest in watching the tiny shrimp swimming around their little dish. I kind of liked showing off my expertise with the microscope, especially to Sarah, who was appropriately impressed. News about my shrimp apparently spread throughout the colony. The interest shown was occasionally startling. Like the time I looked out the kitchen window to see three kids standing there, looking a bit self-conscious, kicking at their own shoes. I recognized two of them as teenagers from the colony, but they were part of a group that didn't hang around with the usual gang of thugs, but kept more or less to themselves. One I recognized by reputation, not to mention appearance. He was probably only seventeen, but he looked thirty. I only knew him as Big Gene. He had a heavy growth of stubble on his face and was wearing a well-worn denim jacket, something that I thought was a bit strange for a warm afternoon in August. He had never spoken to me before this, or even acknowledged my existence, for which I was grateful. I wished my mother was there, or even my sister, but I was alone. Finally, I summoned up the courage to ask in a quavering voice, "What are you doing?" The two other kids looked at Big Gene, who promptly answered, "Nothin'." The adrenaline had kicked in by now, so I followed up with, "What do you want?" Once again, all eyes went to Big Gene, whose major skill apparently wasn't oratory: "Um, uh, well, could we see the shrimp?" I couldn't believe my ears. Immediately shifting gears, I pretended it was a huge inconvenience to let them into my laboratory, but told them "okay" anyway, and in they came. I should have charged admission. With a little assistance from my business associate, Marty, perhaps we could have made another fortune. But no. I let this opportunity go by. Sometimes, we scientists have to put personal gain aside in the interest of the betterment of mankind.

Of far greater importance than my birthday was the Fireman's Ball, held every August at the Hotel Evans. Its major attraction was a big-name orchestra and Hollywood-level entertainment. Tickets had to be purchased far in advance. I even had a special outfit hanging in the closet that wouldn't be touched all summer until that particular evening. It was a sport shirt decorated with graceful palm trees and assorted scenes of the tropics, including a knock-out sunset across the back. I couldn't wait to wear it. Navy blue trousers and dress shoes completed the picture. No sneakers tonight.

Since walking along the road was unacceptable for the Fireman's Ball, we always got a ride from our parents. The girls would have their best dresses on, and would have spent a good part of the day in Pesekow's Beauty Parlor in town getting their hair done. I thought I even detected a hint of perfume as Sarah and I sat together in the back seat of my parents' car. She looked absolutely beautiful and incredibly grown-up in a blue dress I had never seen before, and, sure that my parents couldn't see from their position in the front seat, we held hands all the way to the hotel.

The event itself was in a cavernous ballroom easily five times larger than the Gold Room. All the members of the orchestra were wearing the same red jackets and black trousers; the bandleader's jacket, though, was white, and he had a special spotlight just on him that would follow his every move. The dance floor was crowded with people, and we often found ourselves bumping into other dancers as we moved around the floor. Every now and then, we bumped into Marty and Melanie.

Marty was as scrubbed and polished as I was, and Melanie similarly looked great. We exchanged comments about the orchestra and the other people crowding the dance floor, then made our way back to our respective seats.

The highlight of the evening would be the appearance of the show's star, who usually didn't come on stage until ten o'clock or so. In earlier years, we were never able to stay long enough to be there that late, and would be driven home. But not tonight. After all, I was twelve now. I could hear people murmuring that they had seen him on the Ed Sullivan Show, and one person sitting at a nearby table said that the star had just come from an appearance in Las Vegas. I for one, didn't know who he was, and can't even remember his name, but the adults in the crowd were suitably impressed. He sang quite a few songs, holding a microphone in his hand and walking around the stage as he did so. Every now and then he'd talk to the crowd, ask the hushed audience if they were having a good time, tell a few jokes, and then start singing again. When his time was up, he left the stage accompanied by thunderous applause, waving, bowing, and smiling at the crowd. Then, it was back on the dance floor for just a little while, after which everyone went home, excitedly talking about what a great show and fun evening it was.

Back at Pesekow's, my parents headed for our bungalow, and I walked Sarah home, the sound of chirping crickets our only company. We both had had a wonderful time, all dressed up, looking our best, dancing, talking, laughing, being with someone we each cared so much about. We kissed goodnight, and I slowly walked back up the hill in the quiet of the night.

Before long, my mother tore another page from the calendar hanging on the kitchen wall, and it was September. Labor Day weekend traditionally marked the end of summer, and all around the colony were people carrying all sorts of items out of their bungalows and into their cars. My father parked the Mercury right up next to our bungalow, half on the grass, the first time he had done so since early June. He had been bringing things back home for several weekends, to be sure that everything would fit in the car on the day of our departure for the Bronx. I spent the night before at the casino, saying good-bye to my good friends. Marty and I manfully shook hands, and I exchanged hugs with Melanie, and then with Sarah, who kissed my cheek and said she'd miss me. "Me too," I said, and I meant it. We were still hugging, perhaps a bit too long, so Marty told us to break it up or he'd call the cops. We all wished each other good luck in junior high, where we were all headed, and promised to write, even to Melanie in far away Florida. We had, of course, lived through this scene before, but never at age twelve, which made it all the more meaningful and, in some strange, mysterious way, different. We all looked forward to seeing each other next year, and said our good-byes. There was no sadness. I just walked back up the hill to Bungalow 19, with absolutely no idea that I would never see any of them ever again.

11

Paradise Lost

Not too long ago, there was a faraway place, so far from the steamy streets of the Bronx that a city kid like me was barely able to imagine getting there. And yet, for a precious moment in time, that special place did indeed exist. However, as the world slowly revolved from the 1950s into the 1960s, many of the families who packed up their cars in September and drove back to the city didn't return the following June. So it was with my family. Despite my fervent belief in the notion that sometimes, things should just stay the way they are, time proved itself to be an unstoppable, unopposable force of determined change. Virtually nothing was staying the same. We were encountering changes in our lives that together conspired to push the idea of summer in The Country far out of reach. We had a new apartment in a new borough; I had a new school and some new friends. That first summer in the city was extremely difficult, if not heartbreaking. I couldn't stop thinking about Pesekow's and Loch Sheldrake, Marty, Ray, Melanie, and especially Sarah. I thought about Sarah a lot. I had experienced paradise, and now it was lost.

In The Country, changes were also taking place. With each passing season, the number of vacant bungalows and hotel rooms slowly grew, as did the FOR RENT signs in store windows, and weeds in lawns and playing fields. Soon, those who were not returning far outnumbered those who were. The blueberries ripened on the hill above Loch Sheldrake, and there was no one there to pick them. It didn't take long for the FOR SALE signs to appear. Today, if one were to return to that once-magical land and listen very carefully and intently, one might still hear the voices of the families in the abandoned bungalows, the deserted hotels, the empty casinos. But they would only be echoes, slowly fading into the misty distance.

Time, that unstoppable force of change, continued its relentless work. As the summers went by, what was once the focus of my life eventually was relegated to the realm of memory. Perhaps that is as it was meant to be. For though the experience may have ended, the memory, like the Catskill Mountains themselves, stays forever. And that will never change.

Epilogue

It was just past noon on a cold though sunny April afternoon as I made the left turn onto Route 52 in Woodbourne. It was the first time I had been in the area since we had left for the Bronx that morning in September, 1958. Fifty years had gone by. I wasn't sure why I was there. Some irresistible force had brought me back, unsure of what I'd find, what I'd see. But I knew I had to come. If what remained of the villages of South Fallsburg and Woodbourne were any indication, I wouldn't be seeing very much at all.

As the car climbed the hill towards Loch Sheldrake, I looked up to where the New Roxy Hotel used to be, but it was gone, replaced by a drug rehab center, certainly more a part of today than yesterday. Lake Evans came into view on the left, but the nearby hotel of the same name had similarly vanished, replaced by seemingly endless rows of condos crawling across the slopes and ridges surrounding the lake. An elaborate sign just ahead read ENTERING LOCH SHELDRAKE in flowing gold script, though the shrubbery planted around it had been allowed to grow unchecked, almost obscuring the name of the town just around the bend.

Though I was fully aware of the decline that had occurred in the area over the years, the scene of dilapidation and decay before me was still disheartening. The vibrant little mountain town was little more than a bleached skeleton lying amid the ruins of a war that had been lost. What made it all the more sad was that some of the remaining buildings were still recognizable beneath their rotting facades of plywood and dirt. In what was left of the glassless storefront of the once-tony Town and Country Fashions, I could still see where mannequins once stood, displaying the latest summerwear. Fried's, also minus its plate-glass windows and signage, stood desolate on an empty sidewalk. The theatre, no longer the Strand, apparently had been operating on a limited schedule of unknown design. It had been closed a long time. There was no Sekofsky's, no Herbie's, no Joe's Deli, no Pesekow's Barber Shop and Beauty Salon, no Kove's—in essence, no town. Only the synagogue, next to the theatre, remained unchanged.

I parked the car in a small lot adjacent to an abandoned ice cream stand on the north end of town, across from what used to be Rosenblatt's. Before leaving the car, however, I happened to glance in the rear view mirror, and said aloud to the face looking back at me, "Hey listen, pal, you don't look the same either."

I was parked at the top of a wide sloping lawn that went right down to the water's edge. A sign near the top read BOAT RENTALS BY THE DAY OR HOUR, but of course, it was way too early in the season for boats. I walked down to the water and put my hand in, enjoying the contact. Looking around, I realized that this must be where the woods were between the colony and the boat house, and the path must have run past right where I was standing. If that was the case, then that old cement block of ours must be somewhere nearby, unless it was somehow moved. I started walking along the shore, in what I was certain would be a futile attempt to locate what we sometimes called the Big Rock. But despite all odds, there it was, about thirty feet or so away, amid a patch of weeds that partially hid its location. It seemed to have shrunk and sunk a bit over the years, but otherwise was as I remembered it. How many times had we sat on this block, or stood on it, as I was doing now, talking about its mysterious origins. And this must mean that the colony would have been just another fifty feet or so beyond. As I tried to look through a stretch of leafless brush, shrubs, and trees, I thought

I caught a glimpse of a bungalow colony, though I knew that couldn't be, of course. But it sure looked like it. The brush was too thick to walk through, so I went back up the slope to the road, and walked a bit further north. It didn't take a minute before an unexpected and spectacularly surprising sight was revealed to me.

Like the synagogue, the bungalow colony was actually still there, almost entirely intact. I couldn't believe my eyes. What I thought I saw through the brush a few minutes earlier was absolutely real, and not a mirage. I wondered what incredible quirk of fate saved this island of the past from disappearance. It was amazing, and uplifting, to see. I turned in, and walked past "our" bungalow, up by the road, right next to the first driveway. There was new siding and a new roof, but it looked essentially the same. The number 19, remarkably, was still on the door jamb. The sign that once read L. PESEKOW'S BUNGALOW COLONY was replaced by a smaller one reading LNB PROPERTIES. SALES & RENTALS. I assumed that the colony had been sold at some point in the past, and the bungalows themselves sold off individually as second homes that had been renovated over the years. Their lakeside location had saved them. It was no longer 1958, but, like opening the pages of an old autograph book, I was able to return, in a manner of speaking, to Pesekow's.

I walked around the grounds, letting all the old memories return in a wave of emotion. I felt like that kid just out of sixth grade, arriving in The Country after a long absence: everything around me looked a lot like I remembered it from last time. It felt so good to be back. There was the same spot in the same side-walk where I fell that day running towards the pier. The original pier was gone, replaced by a smaller one, and the casino had been converted into a lakeside home, but the feeling of being there again was the same. There was the basketball court where I used to shoot hoops; the field where we played hide and seek in the darkness; Melanie's house; Marty's bungalow. I walked along under the pines and stopped for a long time in front of what used to be Bungalow 4, lost for a while in the realm of reminiscence . . . *But most of all, remember me.* I stared at a bench between the bungalows and sat down, as I had so long ago. It was in a spot of sun. It was not the same bench, but it was the same sun. I thought about the cross currents that take us through life in this or that direction, the constants and the variables. I leaned back and closed my eyes to the springtime sunshine, grateful for the constants in an ever-changing world.